A Parents ~~Guide~~
to Plym

How to survive and enjoy life in Plymouth with a family

Geraldine Lane

Illustrations by Clair Wyman
Cover design by Maria Lane

Published by Parent Friendly, Plymouth

First published in Great Britain   1983
Second edition   1984
Third edition   1992
Fourth edition   2004

Associated Website: www.parents-guide-to-plymouth.co.uk
e-mail: parentsguide@btinternet.com

ISBN 0 9508813 1 7

British Library Cataloguing in Publication Data

A catalogue record for this book is available from the British Library

Printed in Great Britain by TJ International Ltd. Padstow, Cornwall.

Foreword

I am pleased to be able to welcome this new edition of A Parents Guide to Plymouth. Geraldine Lane has worked patiently over many years to promote effective information services for parents in the city. This guide makes an important contribution to the current network of such services being developed. It links to, and complements the Parent Partnership's Database and Directory of Services for Parenting in Plymouth and the work of the Plymouth Children's Information Service. I am sure it will help parents and carers to find out about what's available in the city for their children and families.

Dr Peter Jones
Educational Psychologist
Manager, Plymouth Parent Partnership Services

ACKNOWLEDGEMENTS

My source of inspiration for the very first edition of A Parents Guide to Plymouth more than twenty years ago is now living in East Anglia, but soon discovered that there is no escape from involvement in this family enterprise, as I owe her a debt of gratitude for her great cover design. Her younger sister once described herself as the marketing tool for Parents Guide. I would like to be able to refute that statement, but I confess that I did indeed pack copies of the first edition in my suitcase when admitted to the Maternity Unit to give birth to her. She would like me to make mention of other events over the years, but I think enough has been said.

There are many people I would like to thank for their assistance and enthusiasm not least my family, but especially my husband whose quiet forebearance and encouragement have kept me going. I am reluctant to list people individually as that leads to the risk of omitting someone, but hope that all those who have helped in any way will accept this as a mark of my gratitude.

Please do tell the advertisers where you read about them, as their support has been essential in the production of the book.

Finally I would like to make special mention of Salinder Supri whose powers of persuasion are responsible for my starting on the long road that has led to this edition, and Sonja Westwood whose invaluable advice kept me on track.

Geraldine Lane
January 2004

The Chelsea Building Society, 169 Armada Way, Plymouth, have kindly sponsored the provision of copies of A Parents Guide to Plymouth to all midwives and health visitors in Plymouth

Change of Lifestyle

by Judy Theobald

"We won't let it alter our lifestyle a bit",
They both say with steadfast intent,
Announcing, with pleasure, to all of their friends
They're expecting a happy event.
"Small children should not disrupt anyone's life,
Should always be seen and not heard."
And of all the people who listen to this,
Not one of them dares say a word.

In due course, the infant appears on the scene,
And true, they've not slept for a week,
They can't sit and chat without baby in arms
But who cares, they can't hear themselves speak
Above all of its screams. They haven't been out
As none of mum's clothes seem to fit,
But they're gritting their teeth and telling the world
It's not changed their lifestyle a bit.

Go back in two years, and the house is all changed,
For gone is the china and glass
Which once graced the sitting room book case and shelves.
Outside in the garden, the grass
Has all disappeared under dollies and prams,
There's wellies and bikes in the hall
And the talk is on potties and nursery schools,
They don't mention lifestyles at all.

A year on, they're all eating jelly for tea,
Brought forward their bedtime to eight,
Their friends never call as they're in the same boat,
And they can't stay awake until late.
But they've wonderful news, they're soon to be joined
By a new little bundle of bounce,
And at least they can say, with no word of a lie,
It won't change their lifestyle an ounce!

(Originally reprinted in "A Parents Guide to Plymouth" from the Western
Morning News with the kind permission of the author)

Copies, including a large print version, of A Parents Guide to Plymouth can be purchased by mail order from Parent Friendly, 21 Ernesettle Crescent, Plymouth, PL5 2ET. Please enquire about discounts for bulk purchase.

Every care has been taken to ensure the accuracy of entries, and Parent Friendly apologise for any errors. Important updates that are brought to our attention will be published on the Internet at www.parents-guide-to-plymouth.co.uk/update.htm. Please copy the form on page 117 to notify any errors, amendments or new information for inclusion in the next edition and on the website.

CONTENTS

Chapter 1: Where to buy or borrow children's things

Chapter 2: Out and about with the family

Chapter 3: Education, day care and leisure

Chapter 4: Family support organisations including health and welfare services

WHERE TO BUY OR BORROW CHILDREN'S THINGS

SHOPPING IN PLYMOUTH

There are a number of shops in the City Centre whose children's departments are not situated on the ground floor. In most cases there is a customer lift but where there is not, always ask the staff to help with prams/ pushchairs - either by allowing you to use the staff lift or by assisting you up and down the stairs. They would rather do this than see people risking an accident on the stairs. A few shops are included from outside the city centre, where they offer something different. Full details are given where a shop is first mentioned. Subsequent entries contain less information.

BABY EQUIPMENT, TOYS, CRAFTS AND HOBBIES

Antics: 30 Royal Parade, Plymouth. Tel: (01752) 221851. Everything to do with model-making plus many craft items, Scalextric, trains and accessories, kites, radio-controlled models and accessories, etc.
Argos Distributors Ltd: Derry's Cross, Plymouth. Tel: (01752) 261975. A free catalogue is available from which goods are purchased in the store. Baby equipment, household and car safety equipment and toys.
Boots: 2 New George Street, Plymouth. Tel: (01752) 266271. Baby equipment; toys; small range of car safety equipment; some household safety equipment; babyfood; toiletries; premature baby nappies. Customer lift. Mother and baby room on ground floor.
Busy Fingers: 123 Cornwall Street, Plymouth. Tel: (01752) 515261. Wide range of craft items – embroidery kits, powder paints, sequin art, etc.
Debenhams: Royal Parade, Plymouth. Tel: (01752) 266666. Toys, baby equipment. Customer lift. Delivery service for which there is a charge. Customer toilets and separate parent and baby room on the third floor.
Derrys Department Store: Co-operative House, Derry's Cross, Plymouth. Tel: (01752) 303030. Prams, cots, travel systems, buggies, Mamas and

1

Papas Premier stockist, rocking horses, car seats, furniture and bedding, safety equipment. Customer lift. Customer toilets, parent and baby room on the second floor. Visit the website at **www.derrys.co.uk**
Dingles: 40 Royal Parade, Plymouth. Tel: (01752) 266611. **¡tridias! toyshop** on the fifth floor. Offer a range of toys and games described as "inventive ideas for children". Customer lift. Customer toilets. Parent and baby room on the fifth floor.
The Disney Store: 51 New George Street, Plymouth. Tel: (01752) 224440. Everything related to Disney marketing. Toys, videos, etc.
Early Learning Centre: 11 Cornwall Street, Plymouth. Tel: (01752) 671206. Devoted to toys, books and activities for all pre-school children, the shop encourages children and parents to 'play-test' the range and runs a free Playtime session every Tuesday morning. Holiday events are organised for children at the Centre. Special terms are available for teachers and playgroup organisers - ask for details. A free catalogue is available and goods may be purchased by mail order. Also have a parent and baby room for breast feeding and nappy changing.
Halfords Superstore: Unit D, Marsh Mills Retail Park, Longbridge Road, Plymouth. Tel: (01752) 224006. Car safety equipment.
Halfords: 15 Cornwall Street, Plymouth. Tel: (01752) 661652. Car safety equipment.
Ham and Sewell: The Armada Centre, Armada Way, Plymouth. Tel: (01752) 253535 Wide range of art and craft materials.
Index Ltd: 51 New George Street, Plymouth. Tel: (01752) 222513. A free catalogue is available from which goods are purchased in the store. Baby equipment, household and car safety equipment and toys.
F.T.B. Lawson: 13 Cornwall Street, Plymouth. Tel: (01752) 665363. Specalist store for tools and cake decorating materials.
Modelzone: 22 Frankfort Gate, Plymouth PL1 1QD. Tel: (01752) 263133. Model kits covering all subjects and for all ages. Radio-controlled boats, cars and planes. Die-cast collectables.
Mothercare: 20 Old Town Street, Plymouth. Tel: (01752) 661423. "Everything for the mother-to-be and her baby and children up to 8". Customer lift. Customer toilets and drinking water machine. Mother's nursing lounge on the top floor and a mum's baby changing room on the ground floor (may be used by dads if free). Delivery service for which a charge is made.
M's Children's Wear: The Pannier Market, Plymouth. Tel: (01752) 254702. Cot bedding.
Patsy Fagan's: in "The House that Jack Built", 11 Southside Street, Barbican, Plymouth, PL1 2LA. Tel: (01752) 252552. Dolls' houses and a wide range of accessories. Also offer a catalogue and postal service.
Plymouth Pannier Market: Entrances in Cornwall Street, New George Street and Market Avenue. A number of stalls sell inexpensive toys, clothes and craft materials.
The School Shop: 67 Ebrington Street, Plymouth. Tel: (01752) 268491. Art and craft materials, toy filling, felt, wadding, display papers and borders, maps and posters.

W.H. Smith: 73 New George Street, Plymouth. Tel: (01752) 669973. Toys and games. Some art and craft materials. Customer lift.

Swings and Roundabouts: "Stroll", Yeoland Lane, Yelverton. Tel: (01822) 852053. Large display of "tp" Activity Garden Toys for sale or hire, e.g. climbing frames, slides, trampolines, paddling pools, garden games sets (croquet, table tennis), pogo stick, etc. Also toy police cars, fire engines, dolls houses, scooters and go-karts.

Teddy's Dolls House and Miniatures: The Retreat, Russell Street, Tavistock, PL19 8BD. Tel: (01822) 612128. Dolls houses and kits, furniture, electrics, papers, etc. Teddies and Dolls Hospital.

The Craft Manual: Unit 21, Saltash Business Park, Moorland Trade Estate, Saltash. Tel: (01752) 847777. Wide range of art and craft and handicraft supplies.

Tom Thumb Miniatures: Dolls houses, furniture and accessories. Plymouth Pannier Market on Saturdays, Plymouth Street Market (in New George Street outside the Pannier Market) on Wednesdays. Tel: (01752) 255193

Toy Box: 149 Fore Street, Saltash, PL12 6AB. Tel: (01752) 848878. Wide range of toys and games for all ages.

Toys R Us: Western Approach, Plymouth. Tel: (01752) 226161. Toys for all ages, nursery furniture, car and household safety equipment. Free parking. Customer toilets with babychange facilities in both male and female. Delivery service for which there is a charge. Customers are not allowed to take shopping bags into the store - they must be left in your car, or they may be deposited in the store's secure area for safekeeping.

Wee Greenies: Tavistock. Tel: (01822) 833584 Independent specialists in WASHABLE NAPPY SYSTEMS. Stockists of Grobags, Bumbo seats, Hippy Chick Hip seats and blankets, organic skin care, lambskins, Muddy Puddles waterproofs, maternity bras and pillows and many more indispensable items for you and your baby. To visit Wee Greenies please telephone for details. Mail order catalogue available.

Woolworths: 66 New George Street, Plymouth. Tel: (01752) 663242. Toys, limited books. Customer toilets on the first floor near the tea bar. There is no lift; a member of staff, if asked, will watch a pram or buggy left on the ground floor if a parent needs access to the toilet. Parent and baby room on the ground floor for nappy changing and breastfeeding.

BICYCLE SALES AND REPAIR

Battery Cycle Works: 52-56 Embankment Road, Plymouth. Tel: 665553. For all ages, starting with tricycles. Accessories, reflective clothing, spares and repairs.

Bike: 2 Pemros Road, St Budeaux, Plymouth. Tel: (01752) 366988. New and second hand bikes, from first size bicycle. Express repair service, accessories, spare parts, reflective clothing.

The Bike Cellar: Unit 1, 11-13 Radford Park Road, Plymstock, Plymouth. Tel: (01752) 408338. Bikes for ages 6 years up. Accessories, spares, repairs, reflective clothing.

Certini Bicycle Co: 10 Kingsmill Road, Tamarview Industrial Estate, Saltash, PL12 6LF. Tel: (01752) 849315. For all ages, starting with tricycles. Accessories, clothing, spares, full workshop facilities. Also have a few second-hand bikes.

Devon Cycles: 2 Frankfort Gate, Plymouth, PL1 1QD. Tel: (01752) 664771. Everything for cyclists of all ages from very young, including trailer bikes and baby seats. Accessories, reflective clothing, spare parts, repairs.

Friends Cycles: 8/10 Stowford Business Park, Ivybridge. Tel: (01752) 690584. For all ages, from tricycles up. Accessories, spares, reflective clothing, repairs. Some second hand bikes.

Halfords Superstore: Marsh Mills, Plymouth. Tel: (01752) 224006. From first bikes. Range of reflective clothing, also spares, accessories, repairs.

Halfords: 15 Cornwall Street, Plymouth. Tel: 661652. From first bikes. Small range of reflective clothing, etc. also spares, repairs, accessories.

Natural Cycles: Benbow Street, Stoke, Plymouth. Tel: (01752) 550729. Sell new and second hand bikes; also offer part-exchange. Range to suit all the family. Very sympathetic to children, offering a measuring service to ensure the bike matches the height of the child. Discount cycles, accessories, spares and reflective clothing.

Plymouth Cycle Scene: Hyde Park House, Mutley Plain, Plymouth. Tel: (01752) 257701. Bikes for all ages, clothing, accessories, same day repairs.

Recycles Mobile Cycle Services

brings bicycle repair to your door or place of work with a free estimation and cost-effective bicycle repair service. Servicing Plymouth and the surrounding area, Recycles owner Alan Pritchard welcomes any queries concerning bicycle repair. email egg104@blueyonder.co.uk or Tel: (01752) 513991

For information on **Cycle Training** see page 79.

BOOKS

Buckfast Abbey Bookshop: Buckfastleigh. Good range of children's religious books. (23 miles from Plymouth city centre)

Christian Literature Centre: The Upper Room, 64 Cornwall Street, Plymouth. Tel: (01752) 66l264. Specialise in religious books.

County Bookshops: 38 New George Street, Plymouth. Tel: (01752) 250777 Constantly changing stock of reduced price remaindered books.

Early Learning Centre: 11 Cornwall Street, Plymouth. Tel: (01752) 671206. Devoted to toys, books and activities for all pre-school children. Have a parent and baby room for breast feeding and nappy changing.

In Other Words: 64 Mutley Plain, Plymouth, PL4 6LF. Tel: (01752) 663889. email: books@inotherwords.co.uk Plymouth's friendly independent bookshop, now situated on two floors. Large section devoted to children's books, with a wide selection from early board books to teenage fiction and non-fiction. Recommendations are readily given - for expert advice, ask for Libby!

W.H. Smith: 73 New George Street, Plymouth. Tel: (01752) 669973. Good range of children's fiction, non-fiction and educational books, including revision guides for GCSE and 'A' level. Customer lift.

The School Shop: 67 Ebrington Street, Plymouth. Tel: (01752) 268491. Educational supplies, including: children's books, Letts Home Study books, Teaching Resources, literacy and numeracy materials, maps and posters.

Waterstones: 65-69 New George Street, Plymouth. Tel: (01752) 256699. Very wide range of children's fiction and non-fiction books, including revision guides for GCSE and 'A' level.

The Works: 86 New George Street, Plymouth. Tel: (01752) 226099. Constantly changing stock of reduced price remaindered books and stationery.

See also Books and Storytelling in the Leisure section in chapter 3.

CAR SAFETY EQUIPMENT

The following table gives a summary of the law relating to the wearing of seat belts by children. Pregnant women are required by law to wear a seat belt if available. The Law states that it is the responsibility of the driver to ensure that children are properly restrained in a vehicle.

An appropriate child restraint is a baby carrier, child seat, harness or booster seat suitable for the child's weight. Approved child restraints must carry the BS "Kitemark" or United Nations "E" mark. A restraint will be labelled by the manufacturers to show the weight for which it has been designed. Some children may find it more comfortable to use a booster cushion (not a household cushion) when wearing an adult belt.

	FRONT SEAT	REAR SEAT
Child under 3 years of age	Appropriate child restraint must be used	Appropriate child restraint must be used if available
Child aged 3 to 11 and under 1.5 metres (approx 5 ft) tall	Appropriate child restraint must be worn if available. If not, an adult seat belt must be worn	Appropriate child restraint must be worn if available. If not, an adult seat belt must be worn if available.
Child aged 12 or 13 or younger child 1.5 metres (approx 5 ft) or more in height	Adult seat belts must be worn if available	Adult seat belts must be worn if available

If there are not enough seat belts available:
The law does not prevent you from carrying more passengers than there are restraints, but available restraints should be used wherever possible. If you have to choose who rides without a restraint, heavier passengers will cause greater injury to others in an accident if they are not wearing a seat belt. If no child restraint is available for children aged under three years of age, it is generally safer for them to wear an adult belt alone, in the back seat, rather than no restraint at all.
(Source of information: Leaflet T/INF251 produced by the Department of Transport 1996)

To find out more about the correct fitting of child car seats and wearing of seat belts, or general road safety information and advice, please contact the Transport & Planning Service, Road Safety Team, Plymouth City Council, Civic Centre, Floor 10, Plymouth, PL1 2EW. Tel: (01752) 307730 or email roadsafety@plymouth.gov.uk.

Car Safety Equipment can be purchased from Car Accessory shops or suppliers of baby equipment (see page 1)

Recently-published advice on purchasing a child car seat:

- Never use a child car seat that has been involved in an accident

- Never buy or use a second-hand child car seat, unless you know its history

- Choose the right car seat for your child's weight, not age

- Ensure the child car seat fits your car

- Ensure the child car seat is fitted properly

- NEVER use a child car seat on a passenger seat fitted with an airbag

CLOTHES FOR CHILDREN

Adams Childrenswear: 17 Cornwall Street, Plymouth. Tel: (01752) 265548. Clothes for children up to 10. Range of clothes for premature babies.

Bay Trading & Co: 59 New George Street, Plymouth. Tel: (01752) 662154. Clothes for girls from 7 years.

BHS: 33 Cornwall Street. Plymouth. Tel: (01752) 667640. Range of children's clothes from birth upwards including basic school uniform items (not school ties, badges, blazers, etc). Parent and baby room for nappy changing and breastfeeding; changing mats in the toilets.

Boots: 2 New George Street. Plymouth. Tel: (01752) 266271. Clothes for babies and young children, including a limited range for premature and low birthweight babies.

Bretagne Marine: 14 Southside Street, The Barbican, Plymouth, PL1 2LA. Tel: (01752) 670045. Children and adults nautical clothing.

B Wise: 80 Royal Parade, Plymouth. Tel: (01752) 254782 Budget price clothes.

B Wise: 2 Victoria Road, St Budeaux, Plymouth. Tel: (01752) 365765 Budget price clothes.

Dance Krazy: 42 Bridwell Road, Weston Mill, Plymouth. Tel: (01752) 363793. Dancewear and clothing for keep fit.

Debenhams: Royal Parade, Plymouth. Tel: (01752) 266666. Range of children's clothes. Customer lift. Customer toilets and separate parent and baby room on the third floor.

Derrys Department Store: Co-operative House, Derry's Cross. Plymouth. Tel: (01752) 303030. Babywear; Grobags, schoolwear department (including school ties, blazers, etc). Customer lift. Customer toilets, parent and baby room on the second floor. Visit the website at **www.derrys.co.uk**

Dingles: 40 Royal Parade. Plymouth. Tel: (01752) 266611. Range of quality children's clothes from birth to 10 years on the fifth floor. Customer lift. Customer toilets. Parent and baby room on the fifth floor.

The Disney Store: 51 New George Street, Plymouth. Tel: (01752) 224440. Everything related to Disney marketing including children's clothes.

JUNEEK

Vast range of Dancewear
Jazz - Ballet - Ballroom
Shoes - Trims - Tights - Gifts
Leotards - Fancy Dress

134 Cornwall Street, Plymouth
Tel: 01752 225943 - closed on Mondays

Amazing prices, amazing selection, amazing service

Etam: 42 New George Street, Plymouth. Tel: (01752) 664144. Girls wear to 16 years upstairs in "Tammy".
Goulds: 57/59 Ebrington Street, Plymouth. Tel: (01752) 665886. Kids Kamouflage jackets, trousers, waistcoats, caps, t-shirts from approx. 5 years. Plus camping gear.
Harlequins Party Shop: 47 Ebrington Street, Plymouth. Tel: (01752) 670640. Fancy dress and costume hire for adults and children. Also accessories, dance wear and alterations.
Jama Uneek: Cornwall Street, Plymouth, PL1 1NJ. Tel: (01752) 225943. Extensive range of children's dancewear from leading makers of quality clothing; shoes and accessories together with wedding shoes, tiaras, gifts, theatrical items and exciting fancy dress. (Closed Mondays)
Kid'z & Co: 59 College Road, Keyham, Plymouth. Tel: (01752) 519738. New branded clothes for 0 - 15 years at bargain prices. Open 9.00 am - 4.30 pm Mon - Fri, 10.00 am - 3.00 pm Sat.
K Sports: Tel/Fax: (01752) 207575. Manufacturers and suppliers of printed and embroidered school wear, sports kits, t-shirts, etc, sold through schools.
Laura Ashley Ltd: Unit B, Armada Centre, Plymouth. Tel: (01752) 268344. Girls clothes from 2 to 9 years.
Littlewoods Stores Ltd: 82 New George Street, Plymouth. Tel: (01752) 662211 Children's clothes from birth to 16 years. Basic school uniform items (not ties, badges, blazers, etc). Customer lift.
Marks & Spencer: 29 Old Town Street, Plymouth. Tel: (01752) 668442. Children's clothes from birth to 14 years, including a full range of boys and girls schoolwear in stock. Customer lift. Offer a 'carry to car' service; goods are held to enable the customer to bring their car to the pick-up point. View the website at **www.marks-and-spencer.com**
Matalan: Transit Way, Plymouth, PL5 3TW. Tel: (01752) 237600. Large range of budget-priced clothing for all ages.
Monsoon: 20 New George Street, Plymouth. Tel: (01752) 600128 Girls' clothes from birth to 14 years.
Mothercare: 20 Old Town Street. Plymouth. Tel: (01752) 661423. Childrenswear from birth to 8 years.
M's Children's Wear: The Pannier Market, Plymouth. Tel: (01752) 254702. Specialists in small birth sizes and christening wear. Clothes from birth to 10 /12 years. Also cot bedding.
National Schoolwear Centre: 105 Mayflower Street, Plymouth. Tel: (01752) 252025. Complete range of uniform (including ties, badges,

sportswear, blazers, etc for 40 schools). Guide and Scout uniforms, Dancewear, embroidery services. Hush Puppy shoes for children.
Next: 22-24 New George Street, Plymouth. Tel: (01752) 667213. Babywear, children's clothes to age 10 years.
One Night Stand: 28 Underwood Road, Plympton, Plymouth. Tel: (01752) 342800. Sell and hire prom dresses, tuxedos and associated accessories.
One Night Stand: 158-160 Fore Street, Saltash. Tel: (01752) 848533. Sell and hire prom dresses and associated accessories.
Pas de Deux: 2 Market Way, Plymouth. Tel: (01752) 603133 Ballet and dancewear, and bridal accessories.
Peacocks: Armada Centre, Armada Way, Plymouth. Tel: (01752) 668732. Children's clothes from birth to 15 years.
Piglets: 120 Fore Street, Saltash. Tel: (01752) 844326. Occasion and casual clothes for children aged 0 - 10 years; low birth weight babywear; schoolwear and shoes; haberdashery and wool.
Plymouth Pannier Market: Entrances in New George Street, Cornwall Street and Market Avenue. Has various stalls selling children's clothes.
Prudence Gowns: 2 Saltash Road, Keyham, Plymouth. Tel: (01752) 558858. Bridal wear.
10's & Under: 104 Embankment Road, Plymouth. Tel: (01752) 214040. New clothing for girls and boys up to 14 years, including Christening, Confirmation, Bridal wear and boys' suits. Monday to Saturday 9.00 am - 4.00 pm.
TK Maxx: 28 Royal Parade, Plymouth. Tel: (01752) 255081. Range of reduced-price clothes and accessories.
Top Drawer Fashions: 23 Morshead Road, Crownhill, Plymouth, PL6 5AD. Tel: (01752) 790095. School uniforms for local schools, principally Eggbuckland and Widey, with ranges in burgundy, blue and green.
Totally Crackers: 15 Beaumont Road, St Judes, Plymouth. Tel: (01752) 663189. Adult and children's fancy dress, costumes made to order, children's dancewear. Visit the website at **www.totallycracker.clara.net**
Toys R Us: Western Approach. Plymouth. Tel: (01752) 226161. Some baby clothes. Customers are not allowed to take shopping bags into

the store - they must be left in your car, or they may be deposited in the store's secure area for safekeeping.

Unique Maternity and Children's Wear: Lower Ground Floor, The Moneycentre, Drake Circus, Plymouth. Tel: (01752) 229806 Independent children's wear shop; clothes for children between 0 and 8 years. Clothes from all over the country, and France and Holland. Stockist of Legowear.

Wilkinson: Armada Centre, Armada Way, Plymouth. Tel: (01752) 255525. A small range of budget children's clothes from birth to 8 years.

Woolworths: 66 New George Street. Plymouth. Tel: (01752) 663242. Children's clothes. Customer toilets on the first floor near the tea bar. **Young Image**: Market Stalls, Plymouth Pannier Market. Tel: (01752) 222527. Children's clothes from birth to 12 years.

MATERNITY WEAR

Boots: 2 New George Street, Plymouth. Tel: (01752) 266271. Maternity bras, pants and tights only.

Derrys Department Store: Co-operative House, Derry's Cross. Plymouth. Tel: (01752) 303030. Underwear/ nursing bras only. Visit the website at **www.derrys.co.uk**

Dorothy Perkins: 18 New George Street, Plymouth. Tel: (01752) 660882/672146. Maternity outerwear and swimwear.

Mothercare: 20 Old Town Street, Plymouth. Tel: (01752) 661423. Full range of maternity wear. Mothers' nursing lounge floor and a mums' baby changing room (may be used by dads if free). Customer lift. Customer toilets and drinking water machine.

Next: 22-24 New George Street, Plymouth, PL1 1RL. Tel: (01752) 667213. Not available in-store, although there is a directory at each till point where customers can browse and order, without obligation, from a full range of maternity wear.

Unique Maternity and Children's Wear: The Moneycentre, Drake Circus, Plymouth. Tel: (01752) 229806. Independent maternity wear shop; stock includes clothes suitable for the professional woman wanting to look smart and feel comfortable during pregnancy. Generous size changing rooms.

Wee Greenies: near Tavistock. (01822) 833584. Supporting You! Maternity/feeding bra fitting service from A - L cup. Stockists include

Bravado and Royce Lingerie. Washable breast pads, silk breast pads, Lansinoh nipple cream and maternity/feeding pillows. Telephone to arrange a fitting. Mail order service also available.

SHOES FOR CHILDREN

Shopping for children's shoes can be a nightmare. The following advice comes from the Association of South West State Registered Chiropodists:

Badly fitting footwear can be so damaging to young feet. Many adult foot problems have their beginnings in the wrong children's and teen's shoes. These rules apply to anyone buying shoes.
• Always have both feet measured for length and width. If the shop can't or won't measure your child's foot, think twice about buying there.
• Remember shoe sizes vary between brands.
• Shoes should be held on the foot with either laces, straps or Velcro. It is best to avoid slip-on shoes.
• Flat shoes are best for children.
• Choose shoes with leather uppers. Synthetics like nylon, plastic and rubber don't allow the sweat to escape properly which increases the chances of athlete's foot and toenail problems.
• The shoe should fit the natural shape of the foot especially around the toes.
• The toe of the shoe should allow toes to move freely and not be squashed from the top or the sides. Make sure there is about 18 mm growing room for children and 1 cm for adults, between the end of the longest toe and the end of the shoe.
• Shoes should fit comfortably around the heel and not be too loose or too tight.
• Socks and tights which are too small can cause similar problems to shoes which are too small, especially in very young children. Knitted bootees and the feet of sleep suits and babygros should be big enough, avoid pram shoes.
• Fashion shoes are fine for special occasions but it is best to wear a more "foot friendly" shoe for regular everyday wear.

There are a number of shoe shops in the city, many offering budget and fashion shoes in single width fittings. The following shoe shops offer shoes in half sizes and several width fittings:

Clarks Shoes Ltd: 42 Cornwall Street, Plymouth. Tel: (01752) 266447. Clarks main agents. Children's shoes are on the first floor. **CFHR*** Customer lift.
Debenhams: Royal Parade, Plymouth. Tel: (01752) 668940. Children's shoe department selling Start-Rite. **CFHR*** Customer lift.
Derrys Department Store: Derry's Cross, Plymouth. Tel: (01752) 303030. Sell Clarks shoes. Customer lift. Visit the website at **www.derrys.co.uk**

*CFHR The Children's Foot Health Register prepares an annual guide which lists those retailers of children's shoes who uphold the standards

fixed by the Management Committee of the Children's Foot Health Register. Copies are available from Children's Foot Health Register, PO Box 249, London, W4 5EX, or visit the Website at www.parents-guide-to-plymouth.co.uk/shoes.htm.

The following shoe makers (outside Plymouth) offer made to measure shoes and can help to solve problems with very narrow/very wide or different size feet:

Conker Shoe Co: 28 High Street, Totnes, TQ9 5RY. Tel: (01803) 862490. Children's and adults' shoes and boots in a range of colours. Telephone for catalogue. Allow about a fortnight for the shoes to be made.

Green Shoes: 69 High Street, Totnes, TQ9 5PB. Tel: (01803) 864997. Children's and adults' shoes, boots and sandals in a range of colours and interesting leathers. Telephone for catalogue. Any width fitting possible, all made to order. Allow up to four weeks for the shoes to be made, although they could be quicker. New, contemporary styles regularly designed. Resoling service and mail order. Also make shoes for vegans.

The following shops offer children's dance shoes:

Dance Krazy: 42 Bridwell Road, Weston Mill, Plymouth. Tel: (01752) 363793

Jama Uneek: 134 Cornwall Street, Plymouth, PL1 1NJ. Tel: (01752) 225943 Closed on Mondays.

Pas de Deux: 2 Market Way, Plymouth. Tel: (01752) 603133

Totally Crackers: 15 Beaumont Road, St Judes, Plymouth. Tel: (01752) 663189. Visit the website at **www.totallycracker.clara.net**.

SPECIALIST SHOPPING

Helping Hands Care Shop: 4 Peverell Park Road, Peverell, Plymouth. Tel: (01752) 228729. Sell equipment and household aids for adults and children with special needs; also items for people who are left-handed. Open Monday to Friday 9.30 am to 4.30 pm.

Plymouth Outdoors: 4 Royal Parade, Plymouth. Tel: (01752) 662614. Sell uniform, equipment, badges, etc for Scouts and Guides.

Mail Order companies:

Anything Left Handed: Specialist mail order company (located in the south east) which provides properly designed, full left-handed versions of over 200 everyday items. Tel: 020 8770 3722 for a catalogue.

Lakeland Ltd: Supply many handy gadgets for those with special needs. Tel: 015394 88100 for a catalogue or list of stores.

SECOND HAND GOODS

Plymouth used to have many small shops which dealt exclusively with second-hand baby equipment, toys, children's and maternity clothes. Sadly most of these appear to have ceased trading. Other ways to obtain second-hand goods are through the classified adverts in the local newspapers, adverts on local radio, car boot sales, jumble sales and sales through local groups, such as mother and toddler groups, playgroups, National Childbirth Trust, etc.

Children's Clothes:
Kid'z & Co: 59 College Road, Keyham, Plymouth. Tel: (01752) 519738. New branded clothes for 0 - 15 years at bargain prices. Open 9.00 am - 4.30 pm Mon - Fri, 10.00 am - 3.00 pm Sat.

Musical Instruments:
Griffin Guitar Centre: 6-8 College Avenue, off Mutley Plain, Plymouth. Tel: (01752) 255121
Maestro's Music Ltd: 52 Ebrington Street, Plymouth. Tel: (01752) 263069. Used musical instruments including brass, woodwind, guitars, percussion, etc.
PD Music: 13 Beaumont Road, Plymouth. Tel: (01752) 267677. Second hand violins.
Plymouth Piano Centre: 77a Upland Drive, Derriford, Plymouth, PL6 6BE. Tel: (01752) 709400. New/ second hand pianos. Visit the website at **www.plymouthpianocentre.co.uk**
Wants Juicy Music: 3 Market Way, Plymouth. Tel: (01752) 664546. Wide range of second hand musical instruments.

Prom Dresses:
One Night Stand: 28 Underwood Road, Plympton, Plymouth. Tel: (01752) 342800. Sell ex-hire prom dresses and unwanted dresses on a 50/50 basis.
Painted Lady: 184 Grenville Road, St. Judes, Plymouth. Tel: (01752) 297338. Sell some second hand prom dresses.
(For second hand Bicycles see page 4)

HIRE AGENCIES
Affordable Fancy Dress: 39 Buckwell Street, Barbican, Plymouth, PL1 2DA. Tel: (01752) 309045. Range of fancy dress costumes and accessories for sale or hire. Will deliver to your home or office.
British Red Cross Society: 60 Crownhill Road, Plymouth. Tel: (01752) 768546. If

there is no answer ring the Devon HQ at Exeter on (01392) 273932. Offer a medical loan service, for items such as wheelchairs, commodes, etc.
Dartmoor Cycles: 6 Atlas House, West Devon Bus Park, Brook Lane, Tavistock (by Safeway) Tel: (01822) 618178. Cycle hire for adults and early teens; kiddy-seats.
Harlequins Party Shop: 47 Ebrington Street, Plymouth. Tel: (01752) 670640. Fancy dress and costume hire for adults and children. Also accessories, dance wear and alterations.
Loopy Looks Costume Hire: 21 Prideaux Close, Tamar View Industrial Estate, Saltash. Tel: (01752) 844789. Costumes and accessories for hire and sale.
One Night Stand: 158 -160 Fore Street, Saltash. Tel: (01752) 848533. Sell and hire prom dresses and associated accessories.
One Night Stand: 28 Underwood Road, Plympton, Plymouth. Tel: (01752) 342800. Sell and hire prom dresses, tuxedos and associated accessories.
Swings And Roundabouts: "Stroll", Yeoland Lane, Yelverton. Tel: (01822) 852053. Bouncy castle, trampolines, play equipment and paddling pool hire.
Theatre Royal: Royal Parade, Plymouth. Tel: (01752) 668282 Costume and fancy dress hire. Visit the website at **www.theatreroyal.com**
Totally Crackers: 15 Beaumont Road, Plymouth, PL4 9BA. Tel: (01752) 663189. Children's and adults' fancy dress and accessory hire. Visit the website at **www.totallycracker.clara.net**
Western Event Hire: 5 Stuart Road, Pennycomequick, Plymouth, PL3 4EA.Tel: (01752) 667999. Cots, high chairs, zed beds and wheelchairs for hire, as well as catering equipment, tables, chairs, etc.
(see also Children's Parties below, for more on children's play equipment hire)

CHILDREN'S PARTIES
Ideas for venues, equipment hire, etc for children's parties. Please ensure that you are satisfied with the insurance arrangements when hiring equipment.

PARTY IDEAS, VENUES, etc
1A Play Away: 57 Bowden Park Road, Crownhill, Plymouth. Tel: (01752) 775186. Bouncy castles, ballpools, soft play shapes, slides for hire for indoor and outdoor parties and fetes.
Absolutely Bouncing Crazy: 125 Church Road, Wembury, Plymouth. Tel: (01752) 863283 Bouncy castles for hire.
Bouncy Bounce Castles: 6 Copse Close, Plymouth, PL7 1QD. Tel: (01752) 348173. Bouncy castle hire with a range for all ages for indoor and outdoor parties.

Celebration Balloons: 63 Weston Park Road, Peverell, Plymouth. Tel: (01752) 251061. Helium filled balloons supplied to decorate a room for a party, as a table centre. Also gift balloons for birth congratulations, birthdays, etc. Range of cuddly toys. Same day local delivery service.

Clay Art: 57 Southside Street, The Barbican, Plymouth. Tel: (01752) 665565 "Paint Your Own Pottery" Cafe. Customers select a piece of pottery, choose a design, and paint. Clay Art provides stamps, stencils, sponges, ideas books, a little coaching and much encouragement. The staff then glaze and fire the piece and it is ready for collection in a few days. Birthday parties a speciality. Visit the website at **www.clayart.co.uk**

CRM Balloons: 91a Mutley Plain, Plymouth. Tel: (01752) 665647 and 131 The Ridgeway, Plympton, Plymouth. Tel: (01752) 337639. Sell helium-filled and foil balloons for all occasions.

Fun-Tasia Inflatables: 255 Blandford Road, Plymouth, PL3 6HT. Tel: (01752) 704350. All types of inflatable rides available for hire for all types of events. Bouncy castles, assault course, football shoot, ball pools, etc.

The Green House Visitors Centre: The Ride, Chelson Meadow, Plymouth, PL9 7JA. Tel: (01752) 482392 Available for birthday parties - offering the hire of a room with tables. The package includes room hire together with full access to the exhibition centre; you can bring your own party food or for an added charge fast food may be pre-ordered and supplied. (see page 24 for further information)

Harlequins Party Shop: 47 Ebrington Street, Plymouth. Tel: (01752) 670640. Fancy dress and costume hire for adults and children. Also accessories, dance wear and alterations.

Jack Cohen's Magic and Joke Shop: 34 Western Approach, Plymouth, PL1 1TQ. Tel: (01752) 667401. Jokes, masks, wigs, hats, fancy dress, accessories, juggling and more.

Jama Uneek: 134 Cornwall Street, Plymouth, PL1 1NJ. Tel: (01752) 225943. Sell an extensive range of exciting fancy dress and theatrical items. Closed on Mondays.

Loopy Looks Costume Hire: 21 Prideaux Close, Tamar View Industrial Estate, Saltash. Tel: (01752) 844789. Costumes and accessories for hire. Also Face Painting.

Marks & Spencer: 29 Old Town Street. Plymouth. Tel: (01752) 668442. Wide range of character and personalised birthday cakes available to order. Customer lift. View the website at **www.marks-and-spencer.com**

Megabowl: Ten pin bowling at two centres: Barbican Leisure Park, Coxside Tel: (01752) 252171 and Plymouth Road, Plympton Tel: (01752) 336666. Ten pin bowling and party menu.

Mr Bounce Bouncy Castles: Tel: (01752) 705812/219508. All sizes of bouncy castles and ball pools for indoor and outdoor use. Also jungle run assault course.

National Marine Aquarium: Tel: (01752) 600301. Offer birthday party trail around the Aquarium followed by a birthday meal in the Ocean View Cafe with a special gift for every child. Check out the Website at **www.national-aquarium.co.uk**

Pennywell Farm: near Buckfastleigh Tel: (01364) 642023 Offers a range of birthday party packages in the special birthday party village. There's a wild west party in a wigwam or a flower fairy or farmyard theme in a woodland log cabin. Visit the website at **www.pennywellfarmcentre.co.uk**

Plymouth Pavilions: Millbay Road, Plymouth. Tel: (01752) 222200. The Birthday Party packages include one activity, a child's meal and a party bag. Check out the Website at **www.plymouthpavilions.com**

The Plymouth Playzone: Christian Mill Business Centre, Crownhill, Plymouth. Tel: (01752) 210210. Family entertainment centre on three floors. Play area, café, bar, party rooms for hire. Ball pools, slides and other play equipment, disco. Food provided as part of party package.

Plymouth Ski Centre: Alpine Park, Marsh Mills, Plymouth, PL6 8LQ. Tel: (01752) 600220. Birthday meal together with a choice of activities from skiing, snowboarding, blading, tobogganing or bobbing. Visit the website at **www.jnll.co.uk/plymouth.php**

South Dartmoor Leisure Centre: St. Leonards Road, Ivybridge. Tel: (01752) 896999. Packages on offer include: I hour swimming OR I hour bouncy castle followed by tea.

Swings and Roundabouts: "Stroll", Yeoland Lane, Yelverton. Tel: (01822) 852053. Bouncy castle, trampolines, play equipment and paddling pool hire; large garden also available for hire for parties for children up to 11, using a range of play equipment set up in the garden. A per head charge is made for the use of the equipment and parents bring their own picnic.

Totally Crackers: 15 Beaumont Road, Plymouth, PL4 9BA. Tel: (01752) 663189. Children's and adults' fancy dress hire at very reasonable rates. Will do face painting, novelties, etc; also sell face paints. Visit the website at **www.totallycracker.clara.net**

Trethorne Leisure Farm: Kennards House, near Launceston. Tel: (01566) 86324. Party packages include meal and visit to farm and activities, plus option of a game of ten pin bowling.

Woodlands Leisure Park: Blackawton, Dartmouth TQ9 7DQ. Tel: (01803) 712598 Private party rooms painted with wacky cartoon characters, hot meals and a full day's play on the many activities.

CHILDREN'S ENTERTAINERS

Billy Whizz the Magician: 17 Okehampton Close, Plympton, Plymouth. Magic shows, balloon modelling, party games. Tel: (01752) 519529.

Funnyfaces Face Painter

Leave your party with a smile on your face – whether it's painted on or not!!

www.funnyfaces.pwp.blueyonder.co.uk
e-mail funnyfaces@blueyonder.co.uk

Tel: 01752 212880

Emazdad the Magician: 24 Haweswater Close, Looseleigh, Plymouth. Tel: (01752) 794159. Children's birthdays, magic shows, balloon modelling, for schools, playgroups.

Fantasy Faces: 11 Fortescue Place, Hartley, Plymouth, PL3 5HT. Tel: (01752) 310463. Face painting specialist and balloonologists. Professionally trained staff are police checked and fully insured. Cater for parties, fundays, fetes, etc - "no job is too big or small!"

Funnyfaces: Tel: (01752) 212880 Face painting for children's parties, events, fetes, corporate events, etc.

Little Box 'partytime' Theatre: Do your children love dressing up and playing make believe? Let them 'act out' a magical tale in your own home or venue, with beautiful costumes to dress up in and a song or two for good measure. Suitable for birthdays and youth groups with children aged 3 years and up. Tel:(01752) 705676 for more details.

Mark's Magic: Tel: 0845 1260354. Children's party specialist, from 20 minutes to the whole day. Birthdays, playgroups, schools, fundays, fetes.

Maunder the Magician: 35 Thornbury Park Avenue, Peverell, Plymouth. Tel: (01752) 228112. Magic entertainment for children's birthdays, playgroups, schools, etc.

Party Time: Tel: (01752) 295653. Children's parties, balloon modelling, face painting, puppet shows, magic.

Pip Critten: Tel: (01752) 361210. Offers "anything and everything" for entertaining children. Magic, string puppet circus, party style disco, balloon modelling, pantomime.

Starlite Disco: 63 Fleet Street, Plymouth. Tel: (01752) 563222. Offer all-inclusive disco for children up to age 11, with light show, bubbles, smoke, party games, etc.

The Storybox Storyteller: Tel: (01752) 569244. A very experienced storyteller and storymaker, specialising in stories for young children and across the primary age range.

BREASTFEEDING FACILITIES IN THE CITY CENTRE

Over the last few years a number of stores have improved their facilities for mothers wishing to feed their babies, although much more could be done. There follows a list of those places where customers can be accommodated, and I would ask that people making use of these facilities please treat them with respect to ensure the continuance of such help as is offered. Provision of customer toilets and babychange facilities is also included.

BHS: 33 Cornwall Street Plymouth. Tel: (01752) 667640. Parent and baby room for nappy changing and breastfeeding, as well as changing mats in the toilets.

Boots: 2 New George Street. Plymouth. Tel: (01752) 266271. Mother and baby room for breastfeeding on the ground floor.

Debenhams: Royal Parade, Plymouth. Tel: (01752) 266666. Customer toilets and separate parent and baby room on the third floor.

Derrys Department Store: Co-operative House, Derry's Cross, Plymouth. Tel: (01752) 303030. Customer toilets and separate parent and baby room on the second floor with bottle/food warmer and nappy dispensing machine. Visit the Derrys website at **www.derrys.co.uk**

Dingles: 40 Royal Parade, Plymouth. Tel: (01752) 266611. Customer lift. Customer toilets. Parent and baby room on the fifth floor.

Early Learning Centre: 11 Cornwall Street, Plymouth. Tel: (01752) 671206. Parent and baby room for breast feeding and nappy changing.

Mothercare: 20 Old Town Street, Plymouth. Tel: (01752) 661423. Customer lift. Customer toilets and drinking water machine. Mothers' nursing lounge on the top floor and a mums' baby changing room on the ground floor (may be used by dads if free).

Plymouth Railway Station: Saltash Road. Baby changing room next door to the Ladies toilets on platform 2, which is available to mums and dads.

Toys R Us: Western Approach, Plymouth. Tel: (01752)226161. Customer toilets with babychange facilities in both male and female.

Woolworths: 66 New George Street, Plymouth. Tel: (01752) 663242. Parent and baby room on the ground floor for nappy changing and breastfeeding. Customer toilets on the first floor near the tea bar. There is no lift; a member of staff, if asked, will watch a pram or buggy left on the ground floor if a parent needs access to the toilet.

PUBLIC CONVENIENCES (City Centre and Foreshore)

A number of shops have toilets and these are mentioned in their entry earlier in this chapter.

Armada Way – at the junction of Armada Way and New George Street

Bretonside Bus Station

Tavistock Road, beside the City Museum.

Barbican - at Phoenix Wharf and beside the Barbican Glass Works
The Hoe Promenade – at the east end beside the Park Keeper's Lodge
West Hoe – situated at the park at the west end of Madeira Road

These all have compartments for use by disabled persons and are part of
the RADAR key scheme; The RADAR key is part of a nation-wide
scheme, and will open toilets across the EU. There is a small charge of £4
for the keys and you will be required to provide proof of
disability/requirement for use (eg. Disability Living Allowance, Disabled
Persons Registration SS310, Blue Badge or Letter from GP/consultant).
They are available from:
Plymouth Guild of Community Service, Ernest English House, Buckwell
Street, Plymouth, PL1 2DA, Tel: (01752) 201766 and First Stop, Plymouth
City Council, Civic Centre Plymouth PL1 2EW Tel (01752) 668000,
Minicom 01752 264 946 or 01752 304 577

CONSUMER ADVICE

Citizen's Advice: Virginia House, 40 Looe Street, The Barbican,
Plymouth. Tel: (01752) 207088. Open Monday 10.00 am - 3.00 pm,
Tuesday 10.00 am - 1.00 pm, Thursday 10.00 am - 3.00 pm. Free advice.
See entry in Chapter 4.

Plymouth City Council Trading Standards: Tel: (01752) 304580 or
304581. Functions include the inspection of various articles, including
toys, baby equipment, etc, to see if they conform to descriptive claims or
legal standards of quality and safety. Offer a free advice service.

OUT AND ABOUT WITH THE FAMILY

TOURIST ATTRACTIONS

The following pages give details of many of the tourist attractions in the region of particular appeal to families. Many places offer reduced rates for parties and out of season visits. Telephone numbers are given (where available) and it is advisable to check current opening times and admission charges with the attraction, before setting out. National Trust historic houses do not admit dogs (except guide dogs), prams, pushchairs or backpack baby carriers (although some offer the loan of front-sling baby carriers). There are also many walks, nature trails, coastal footpaths, woods and forests which can be explored free of charge – details of some of these can be found later in this chapter or from the Tourist Information Centres (see page 36).

Walks and Visits in Plymouth

These are some of the many attractions in easy reach of Plymouth city centre. City Centre representatives are Plymouth's on-the-street source of tourist information and assistance. They patrol the city centre wearing their distinctive green uniforms.

PLYMOUTH HOE
Large grass area with superb views across **Plymouth Sound**, with its constantly changing panorama of ships and small boats. **West Hoe Fun Park** offers crazy golf, trampolines, and mini-marina with radio-controlled boats, miniature railway and giant airbed. A sensory garden on Plymouth Hoe has been designed with the visually impaired in mind.

Plymouth Dome: Hoe Road, Plymouth, PL1 2NZ. Tel: (01752) 600608 for recorded information on opening hours and prices. Tel: (01752)

603300 for bookings. An award winning visitor centre for all the family, covering the history and geography of Plymouth from Elizabethan Times to the present day, in various formats from audio visual to interactives,with a display on Lighthouses of the Eddystone Rock. Disabled friendly; family friendly. Save money by purchasing a 'heritage passport' to various other venues throughout the area. View the website at **www.plymouthdome.info**

Smeaton's Tower is probably Plymouth's most famous landmark. It was a functional lighthouse - originally built on the Eddystone Rock in 1759 and rebuilt on Plymouth Hoe in 1884, it has recently undergone extensive refurbishment, with a related exhibition at Plymouth Dome. (A word of caution: be aware that it has the steep winding stairs associated with such structures!). Tel: (01752) 600608 for recorded information on opening times and prices. Save money by purchasing a 'heritage passport' to various other venues throughout the area. Open end of March to end of October.

The **Royal Citadel** on Plymouth Hoe has great views of the city's waterfront from the 17th century ramparts. Also historic cannons and the peaceful chapel of St. Katherine. Tel: (01752) 775841. Tickets available from Plymouth Dome and The Tourist Information Centre on the Barbican (see page 36).

Waterfront walkway: Easy to follow route for all the family and all abilities, around the Hoe and Barbican. Walkers' guides and audiotapes are available from the Tourist Information Centres. The guide features "Kids' Corners" in many sections with puzzles designed to make the walkway fun for the young. Pleasure boats operate from here with a choice of trips up the River Tamar as far as Calstock, around Devonport Dockyard, around the coast to the River Yealm or around the harbour with a visit to the National Marine Aquarium.

PLYMOUTH BARBICAN
This is the historic heart of the city, where the Mayflower memorial commemorates the departure of the Pilgrim Fathers for the New World. It is a mix of cobbled streets, fishing boats, art galleries, and old buildings which escaped the ravages of the war.

Barbican Glassworks: The Old Fishmarket, The Barbican. Tel: (01752) 224777. Operated by Dartington Crystal, the Glassworks produces its own range of glassware in Torrington using recycled glass. From time to time there are exhibitions relating to the locality in the gift shop.

Clay Art: 57 Southside Street, The Barbican. Tel: (01752) 665565 **"Paint**

Your Own Pottery" Cafe. Adults, teens and children of all ages are welcome to drop in at any time the studio is open. Customers select a piece of pottery, choose a design and paint. Staff then glaze and fire the piece and it is ready for collection in a few days. Open Tuesday to Sunday. Group bookings and birthday parties by arrangement. Visit the website at **www.clayart.co.uk**

Elizabethan House: Tel: (01752) 304774 for details. Built in the late 16th century, it is located in New Street immediately behind the Island House, on the Barbican. An Elizabethan sea-captain's house complete with real Tudor furnishings. Save money by purchasing a 'heritage passport' to various other venues throughout the area. Small entrance charge. Concession for children; under 7 years free.

Merchants House: Situated on the west side of St. Andrew's Street, immediately south of the Magistrate's Court. This 16th Century Jacobean town house is a museum of Plymouth's social history, containing much that appeals to children, including model ships and a furnished Victorian doll's house. In the Apothecary's Room the contents (some over 200 years old) of the former Mutley Plain pharmacy of C.J. Park have been carefully arranged to give the atmosphere of an olde-worlde chemists shop. Save money by purchasing a 'heritage passport' to various other venues throughout the area. Small entrance charge. Concession for children; under 7 years free.

22

Mount Batten Peninsula is just a 5 minute boat ride away from the Barbican. Formerly belonging to the Ministry of Defence, and now redeveloped, there is access to the coastal footpath; also waterside events, breakwater promenade, pub and waterfront tower.

National Marine Aquarium: The Barbican. Tel: (01752) 600301 Contains one of the finest collections of marine animals in Europe, including a 2.5 million litre shark tank and a feature on the world of seahorses. Europe's deepest aquarium tank can be viewed near the surface, mid-water and from the sea bed. There is a new walk through demi tunnel; also underwater shipwreck . . and more. Meet Snorkel the Loggerhead Turtle and Bentley the strange-looking Humphead Wrasse. Come and see **Roboshark** - the robotic shark that's programmed with a mind of its own to come face to face with the real sharks. There are daily talks right through the year. Parties admitted at special rates. Open all year except Christmas Day. Entrance tickets can be purchased from Tourist Information Centres. Wheelchair access to all displays. Visit the Website at **www.national-aquarium.co.uk**

PLYMOUTH CITY CENTRE

Plymouth City Museum and Art Gallery: Drake Circus. Tel: (01752) 304774 or email plymouthmuseums@plymouth.gov.uk. Collections of paintings, porcelain, local history. Children will probably be most interested in the well set out natural history section on the ground floor. Tuesday to Friday 10.00 am - 5.30 pm, Saturday 10.00 - 5.00 pm. Admission free. There are often interesting exhibitions on the first floor. Baby change facilities. Level access for wheelchair and pushchair users at the rear entrance in Tavistock Place. Lift and wheelchair available on request. Art exhibitions have been made more accessible to partially-sighted visitors, with the provision of an audio guide. It is advisable to phone in advance to aid staff in ensuring a smooth visit if access is a problem for you.

Plymouth Pavilions: Millbay Road. Tel: (01752) 222200. Has something for everyone with a skating rink, swimming pool, brand new eating area and many varied shows in the large concert arena. Check out the Website for more information at **www.plymouthpavilions.com**

Accessible by foot ferry from Plymouth City Centre:
Mount Edgcumbe House and Country Park: Cremyll, Torpoint, Cornwall. Tel: (01752) 822236. The house is a restored Tudor mansion standing in magnificent parkland with superb views of Plymouth Sound which can be reached on foot via the Cremyll Pedestrian Ferry operating from Admiral's Hard (off Durnford Street, Stonehouse) or by car via the A374 and B3247 from the Torpoint Ferry. A ferry timetable is available at the Cremyll

tollgate. Telephone enquiries about the ferry can be made on (01752) 822105. For further information see page 44.

PLYMOUTH ATTRACTIONS OUTSIDE THE CITY CENTRE

Crownhill Fort: Crownhill Fort Road, PL6 5BX. Tel: (01752) 793754 Crownhill Fort is the largest and most important of Plymouth's great Victorian forts built in the 1870's to defend Plymouth from attack by land as well as sea. Today it is fully open for you to explore and is a great family day out with a junior agility challenge (with its very own miniature fort), an indoor activity centre, dressing up for children and a daily gun-firing at 1.30pm by costumed staff. The maze of tunnels and passages that make up the Fort are full of sound effects re-creating the shouts and sounds of a Victorian Fort in action. And there are trails for all ages – which ensure every corner of the Fort is fully explored! 4 miles from Plymouth City Centre on the A386 Tavistock Road. Visit the website at **www.crownhillfort.co.uk**

Green House Visitor Centre: The Ride, Chelson Meadow. Tel: 482392. "The first leisure-based sustainable waste education exhibition" it includes a cave hiding outsize versions of waste items, aimed at teaching about waste disposal in a fun way. See the largest recycled bottle glass window in the UK. Open Tuesday to Saturday 10 am - 5 pm (last admission 4.00 pm).The Centre is also available for birthday parties and conference hire. Free parking. On the A379, follow the signs for Chelson Meadow.

Hemerdon House: Plympton, Plymouth Tel: (01752) 337350. Furnished Georgian family home, open 30 afternoons per year between May and September.

Plym Valley Railway: Marsh Mills Station, Plymouth, PL7 4TB. The aim of the railway is to preserve steam and diesel locomotives and rolling stock and buildings, machinery and equipment of historic railway interest. Follow the brown train signs off Marsh Mills roundabout (Plympton) and the Railway is opposite the Coypool Park and Ride car park. Open most Sundays from 11.00 am.

24

Plymbridge Woods: 124 acres of the wooded valley of the River Plym, owned by the National Trust. There are bathing and picnic places beside the river. No admission charge. Access from Estover or Plympton via Plymbridge Lane.

Plymouth Naval Base Museum: Devonport Naval Base Tel: (01752) 554200 (Visitors Office) or (01752) 554582 (Museum Reception Office). At present only pre-arranged visits by groups can be accommodated, by appointment for the purposes of security clearance. Contains an impressive collection of ship models, mostly covering the last one hundred years. Large collection of artefacts from the Royal William Victualling Yard which closed in 1992 after 150 years supplying provisions to the Royal Navy. Also books, documents, photographs and plans relating to the Dockyard and the ships stationed there over the last 300 years. The Museum will open to the public when the visitor centre is completed.

Tamar Bridges The car park at theTamar Bridge enjoys wonderful views up and down the river, including Brunel's magnificent railway bridge and the Tamar road bridge which link Devon and Cornwall; information on the road bridge is available from the Bridge office at the car park.

Saltram House: Plympton, Plymouth, PL7 1UH. Tel: (01752) 333500. (National Trust) A magnificent Georgian mansion, complete with its original

furniture and paintings. Features include a children's room with a furnished 18th century dolls' house and clothes for children to dress up. Admission to either the House and Garden or Garden only. It is set in a lovely landscaped park overlooking the Plym estuary. Free admission charge to the park which is open all year round. House open daily (except Fridays) 12 noon – 4.30 pm end of March to end of September, 11.30 - 3.30 pm in October (last entry 30 minutes before closing - end March to end October). Saltram is situated 4 miles east of the city centre on the west side of Plympton, between the A38 and A379. Visit the website at **www.nationaltrust.org.uk**

The Evening Herald and Radio Devon regularly give information on the movement of Royal Naval ships into and out of the Dockyard. Take the opportunity to go to vantage points like the Hoe, Mount Edgcumbe and Devil's Point to watch the ships. See also Nature Reserves on page 46.

DEVON

Babbacombe Model Village: Hampton Avenue, Babbacombe, Torquay, TQ1 3LA Tel: (01803) 315315 Impressive model village with miniature landscaped gardens and an evening light spectacular. (34 miles from Plymouth city centre)

Becky Falls Woodland Park: Manaton, near Bovey Tracey on the east side of Dartmoor. Tel: (01647) 221259. A variety of trails through the woods, marked in different colours, from easy strolls to very demanding. Discovery trails for children. Stout walking shoes are recommended for the walk to the falls. (33 miles from Plymouth city centre). Visit the website at **www.beckyfalls-dartmoor.com**

Berry Pomeroy Castle: Berry Pomeroy, near Totnes. Tel: (01803) 866618. One of the largest castles in Devon, it dates from Norman times, with dungeons and the ruins of a never-completed Tudor mansion. Said to be the most haunted castle in Devon. Refreshments; 2.5 miles east of Totnes off A385. (25 miles from Plymouth city centre)

Bowden House: Totnes, TQ9 7PW Tel: (01803) 863664. Houses the British Photographic Museum. Tudor House (reputed to be haunted); children's corner, refreshments. Guides dress in Georgian costume. 1 mile from Totnes on A361. (24 miles from Plymouth city centre)

Buckfast Abbey: Buckfastleigh. Tel: (01364) 645500. Built over a period of 32 years, being completed in 1938 by Benedictine Monks who made the monastery their home. The Abbey is a very beautiful building - visitors are asked to respect the fact that it is a church and dress and behave accordingly. Other features include an award-winning education service, shops, tea rooms, a very comprehensive religious book shop, information office. Mother and baby room. (23 miles from Plymouth city centre)

Buckfast Butterfly Farm and Dartmoor Otter Sanctuary: Buckfastleigh, TQ11 0DZ. Tel: (01364) 642916. Butterflies from all over the world in a jungle habitat; otters in a carefully-designed environment. Also birds, fish and terrapins. (23 miles from Plymouth city centre)

Buckland Abbey: Yelverton, PL20 6EY. Tel: (01822) 853607. Once a Cistercian monastery, then the home of Sir Richard Grenville who sold it to Sir Francis Drake; now jointly managed by the National Trust and Plymouth City Council. It contains many Elizabethan artefacts and details much of Drake's history. Way marked walks through 600 acre estate. Family activities often arranged in school holidays. Situated 11 miles north of Plymouth off the A386. Managed jointly by the National Trust and Plymouth City Council. Visit the website at **www.nationaltrust.org.uk**

Burrator: Dartmoor. Many attractive walks in the woodlands surrounding Burrator Reservoir. Leave Plymouth on the A386 Yelverton road, from Yelverton follow the B3212 to Dousland, then follow the signs for Burrator.

Canonteign Falls: Chudleigh Tel: (01647) 252434. Said to be England's highest waterfall at 220 feet. Woodland walks, Wetland Nature Reserve, adventure playgrounds, picnic sites. (33 miles from Plymouth city centre)

Cardew Teapottery: Newton Road, Bovey Tracey, TQ13 9DX. Tel: (01626) 832172 Home of the world's most extraordinary teapots. Activity centre based on the theme of Alice in Wonderland. Lake with ducks; tea room. (32 miles from Plymouth city centre)

Coldharbour Mill Working Wool Museum: Uffculme, Cullompton, EX15 3EE. Tel: (01884) 840960. Discover the story of the Victorian adults and children who worked here! See how low children crawled under working machinery and find out how noisy a power loom was. Mill shop, restaurant and picnic area. (62 miles from Plymouth city centre)

Crealy Adventure Park: Sidmouth Road, Clyst St Mary, Exeter, EX5 1DR. Tel: (01395) 233200. With the first log flume in Devon; also action, adventure, animal, farming, magic and natural realms. (47 miles from Plymouth city centre)

Dartmoor's Miniature Pony and Animal Farm: On Dartmoor 2 miles west of Moretonhampstead on the B3212. Tel: (01647) 432400. Over 150 animals including miniature ponies and donkeys that foal throughout the spring and early summer, on 20 acres of Dartmoor parkland. Picnic area; restaurants; courtyard of shops, gallery and cafe. (38 miles from Plymouth city centre)

Dartmoor National Park: The National Park Authority organise guided walks and events, some of which are specifically designed for young people and families. The walks are led by knowledgeable guides who are all Dartmoor enthusiasts. If you have any doubts talk to the guides before setting off. Final walking routes will be decided by the guide, taking into account the weather and ability of the group. There are guided tours in the summer for people with disabilities - further details available on (01752) 690444. Copies of the free Dartmoor Visitor newspaper, containing details of walks and other events, are available from the National Park Information Centres. For further information about Dartmoor telephone/visit the High Moorland Visitor Centre at Princetown on (01822) 890414. See page 65 for a related children's activity group.

Dartmoor Wildlife Park: Sparkwell, near Plympton. Tel: (01752) 837645. Over 150 species of animals and birds, mainly in large enclosures, set in 30 acres. Pony rides; falconry displays; walk-in enclosure with animals and birds; picnic area; restaurant. (9 miles from Plymouth city centre)

Diggerland: Verbeer Manor, Cullompton, EX15 2PE. Tel: 08700 344437. Where adults and children can drive real JCBs; plus other activities. (63 miles from Plymouth city centre)

Dingles Steam Village: Lifton. Tel: (01566) 783425. Working and static exhibits of steam engines and vintage machinery, bringing Britain's industrial heritage to life.

Kitley Caves: Yealmpton. Tel: (01752) 880885. Evidence of stone age man, mammoth, hyena and cave bear can be seen in the Interpretation Centre. Lime kilns; scenic woodland and riverside walks with picnic areas; adventure play areas. (7 miles from Plymouth city centre)

Living Coasts: Beacon Quay, Torquay, TQ1 2BG. Tel: (01803) 202470. Family adventure and a chance to find out about marine conservation. (32 miles from Plymouth city centre)

Morwellham Quay Open Air Museum: Tavistock. Tel: (01822) 832766. A 19th century copper mine and picturesque old port. Visitors can ride the woodland tramway beside the River Tamar and into the copper mine. Try on 1860's costumes and watch fascinating demonstrations (seasonal). Explore the quays, Garlandstone ketch, cottages, farm, museums, school and workshops. Wildlife Reserve, woodland and riverside trails; picnic parks, Victorian Inn (seasonal). Allow 4 – 5 hours for a visit. Follow signs from Plymouth to Tavistock then A390. A season ticket is available allowing, on payment of a yearly fee, unlimited visits and reduced price admission to special events at Morwellham. (14 miles from Plymouth city centre) Visit the website at **www.morwellham-quay.co.uk**

Overbecks Museum and Garden: Sharpitor, near Salcombe. Tel: (01548) 842893. (National Trust) A six-acre garden with rare plants and shrubs, with spectacular views over Salcombe estuary. Museum of ships, shipbuilding, local shells, moths, butterflies, birds' eggs, animals. Children's room with exhibition of dolls and toys. 100 year old Polyphon. Picnic area; light refreshments available. Closed on Saturdays. Situated 1.5 miles from Salcombe, signposted from Marlborough and Salcombe. (24 miles from Plymouth city centre)

Paignton Zoo Environmental Park: Totnes Road, Paignton. Tel: (01803) 527936 (Information line) or (01803) 697500. Large zoo, involved in conservation breeding programmes, with gardens, nature trail, family activity centre and miniature railway. The Zoo's Education Service, which has classrooms, a library and a loan service of educational materials, welcomes educational visits. Refreshments; Mother and baby room. (28 miles from Plymouth city centre)

Parke Rare Breec collection of rare b interpretation cen† Bovey and unspo city centre)

CLOSED DOWN

T~l· (01626) 833909. A ' corner, rabbit village, Valks along the River miles from Plymouth

Pennywell Farm: near Buckfastleigh Tel: (01364) 642023. The big all day farm fun and activity park. Farm craft and wildlife activities to entertain the family all day. Race the ferrets, bottle feed the baby lambs or enjoy a puppet show and sing-along in the Farmyard Theatre. A different hands-on activity every half hour; listen for the bell. Nativity plays and visits to Santa during December. (24 miles from Plymouth city centre) Visit the Website at **www.pennywellfarmcentre.co.uk**

Prickly Ball Farm Hedgehog Hospital: Prickly Ball Farm, Denbury Road nr Newton Abbot, TQ12 6BZ. Tel: (01626) 362319. Once in Newton Abbot follow the signs to Totnes which will take you onto the A381, follow this road for about 1 mile. Go straight ahead at the roundabout and turn right after 40 metres into Denbury Road. Continue for half a mile until you find the car park on the left. (34 miles from Plymouth city centre)

River Dart Adventures: Holne Park, Ashburton. Tel: (01364) 652511. 90 acres of parkland, woodland, with riverside and nature trails. Extensive adventure playgrounds, and Pirate ship in Smugglers Cove play lake with toddlers beach. Picnic areas and refreshments. In the school holidays organised day activities include climbing, caving and canoeing. Also 'Dare Devil' activities for all the family, including high ropes, mega zip wire, canoeing and indoor climbing (at small extra cost). (24 miles from Plymouth city centre)

Salcombe Chocolate Factory: Orchard Court, Island Street (next to Salcombe Dairy Ice Cream). Tel: (01548) 842260. See chocolates being made in this factory outlet, with gift shop. (23 miles from Plymouth city centre)

Sorley Tunnel Adventure Farm: Loddiswell, near Kingsbridge. TQ7 4BP. Tel: (01548) 854078 Sorley tunnel offers a full days entertainment for the children and the chance for the whole family to participate in the activities of a fully organic farm. Horse riding is offered in a purpose built barn. (21 miles from Plymouth city centre)

South Devon Steam Railway: The Station, Buckfastleigh, TQ11 0DZ. Tel: 0845 345 1466 Steam trains running on the old GWR branchline from Buckfastleigh to Totnes from April to October. Phone for railway timetable. Set in several acres of grounds with picnic areas; children's play area and maze, museum, stock shed, model railway, refreshments. Also Santa trains at weekends in December. (23 miles from Plymouth city centre)

Woodlands Leisure Park: Blackawton, Dartmouth TQ9 7DQ. Tel: (01803) 712598. 60 acre park with a variety of rides and outdoor action-packed zones. Five floor indoor venture centre; picnic areas; mother and baby room. 4 miles from Dartmouth on the A3122. (32 miles from Plymouth city centre)

Other attractions in Devon may also be found detailed in the free "Holiday Times" newspapers for South Devon and South Hams, available from Tourist Information Offices.

CORNWALL

The Cornwall Tourist Board can be contacted by telephone on (01872) 322900.

Antony House: Torpoint Tel: (01752) 812191. (National Trust) 18th century house, superb woodland and formal gardens. Antony is only open in the afternoon 1.30 - 5.30 pm on certain days, although the Woodland Garden (not National Trust) is open daily from 11.00 to 5.30 pm. Tea room. (5 miles from Plymouth city centre via Torpoint Ferry)

Bodmin and Wenford Steam Railway: Bodmin General Station, Bodmin, PL31 1AQ. Tel: 0845 1259678. Running from Bodmin General to Bodmin Parkway the steam railway is a nostalgic trip through the Cornish countryside. Runs through the summer with Santa specials at Christmas. (31 miles from Plymouth city centre)

Carnglaze Caverns: Near Liskeard Tel: (01579) 320251 A former slate mine, with three huge caverns. One of these (the Rum Store) is used as a concert venue. The 6.5 acre site also features walks through woodlands and beside rivers and streams and an enchanted dell with bronze statues of fairies. Also a craft centre with a 500-piece collection of minerals from the south-west. (20 miles from Plymouth city centre)

Cotehele House: Near Calstock Tel: (01579) 351346. (National Trust) A Tudor mansion on the banks of the Tamar. The house contains its original Tudor armour, furniture, tapestries and needlework. The valley garden has a dovecote and fishpond; there is also a watermill together with shipping museum, blacksmith's forge, wheelwright's shop, slide show, quay and restored Tamar barge, "Shamrock". Programme of family holiday activities, quizzes and trails. Phone for details. Parents and babies room. Light refreshments. (15 miles from Plymouth city centre)

Dobwalls Family Adventure Park: Dobwalls Tel: (01579) 320325. Two miniature western railroads based on the American railroad system. Unlimited train rides and indoor and outdoor children's play areas. (22 miles from Plymouth city centre)

The Eden Project: Bodelva, St Austell, PL24 2SG. Tel: (01726) 811911. Described as the Eighth Wonder of the World, two gigantic domed conservatories (biomes) are full of plants from all over the world. (35 miles from Plymouth city centre).

Flambards Theme Park: Helston Tel: 0845 601 8684 Large range of activities, rides and exhibits, including The Victorian Village and Britain in the Blitz. (70 miles from Plymouth)

Colliford Lake Park: St Neot, Liskeard, PL14 6PZ. Tel: (01208) 821469. Spacious moorland park, at the heart of Bodmin Moor, with views of Colliford Lake. Large undercover play area themed on North Cornwall; indoor and outdoor picnic areas; rare breed and indigenous animals; electric racing and agility cars, eco karts; paintball range; miles of woodland and wetland walks; drop slide, zip wires, astro slide; refreshments. (24 miles from Plymouth).

Goonhilly Satellite Earth Station: Helston, TR12 6LQ. Tel: 0800 679593. On the B3293 Helston to St Keverne road, about 7 miles from Helston. Discover the largest satellite station on earth. With multimedia visitor's centre, interactive exhibits, guided tour, journey through the history of international satellite communication, film show, Internet facilities, satellite dishes you can move yourself. Admission is free for Devon and Cornwall schools. Curriculum link resources for key stage 2,3 and 4. Open all year for school group bookings. Picnic and play areas, café, shops. (67 miles from Plymouth)

Hidden Valley Discovery Park and Garden Railways: Tredidon, St Thomas, Launceston, PL15 8SJ. Tel: (01566) 86463 Two garden railways with five working trains; the crystal challenge – solve the clues and get a "crystal"; new for 2004 – Catastrophe Creek – a train ride into a canyon with surprises! Discovery trails, lakeside walks; children's play area; picnic area, tea room; shop. Open mid-April to September. Located 4 miles west of Launceston, signposted from the A395.

Launceston Steam Railway: Tel: (01566) 775665. Narrow gauge steam railway using closed and open carriages on a five mile round trip through the Kensey Valley. Workshop, museum, bookshop, gift shop. Picnic area; refreshments. Open during the tourist season; closed on Saturdays. Access via Newport Industrial Estate, Launceston. (off A388 Bude/ Holsworthy road). (26 miles from Plymouth).

Mary Newman's Cottage: Saltash. A cottage dating from the 1450's reputed once to have been the home of Mary Newman, first wife of Sir Francis Drake. It has been restored with period furnishings by the Tamar Protection Society. Watch the local press for opening times and special exhibitions. (6 miles from Plymouth city centre)

The Monkey Sanctuary: Tel· (01503) 262532. Come and meet a colony of woolly monkeys. Regular talks on the life of the monkeys, together with the opportunity to watch a colony of lesser horseshoe bats roosting in the cellar. There is a variety of children's activities, including a play area and activity room. Park area and vegetarian cafe. Situated off the Plymouth - Looe road (B3253). Open April to September, Sunday to Thursday, 11.00 am to 4.30 pm and Autumn half term. (20 miles from Plymouth city centre)

Mount Edgcumbe House and Country Park: Cremyll, Torpoint, Cornwall. Tel: (01752) 822236. The house is a restored Tudor mansion standing in magnificent parkland with superb views of Plymouth Sound (see page 23 for full details)

National Maritime Museum Cornwall: Discovery Quay, Falmouth, TR11 3QY Tel: (01326) 313388 Interactive and hands on displays, maritime heritage, cafe and shop. Open daily 10.00 am to 5.00 pm except Christmas Day and Boxing Day and 5th - 30th January 2004. (68 miles from Plymouth)

Paul Corin's Magnificent Music Machines: St Keyne Station, near Liskeard. Tel: (01579) 343108 See and hear instruments dating from the Victorian era through to the 1930's, including Belgian cafe organs, polyphon, orchestrion, Mighty Wurlitzer Theatre Pipe Organ, etc. set in a tranquil old mill in the lovely Looe Valley. Picnic area by the river; dogs on leads. Open daily 10.30 am to 5.00 pm until the end of October. Follow the B3254 from Looe or Liskeard, or by train from Looe or Liskeard to St Keyne Station (request stop). (19 miles from Plymouth city centre).

Porfell Animal Land Wildlife Park: Trecangate, nr Lanreath, Liskeard, PL14 4RE. Tel: (01503) 220211 Familiar animals and some different ones. Rabbits, goats, ducks, chickens, deer and five different species of lemur in the newly opened Lemurland. Open daily 10.00 am to 6.00 pm until the end of October. From Looe and Polperro take the A387, turn for Liskeard on the B3359 through Pelynt, past the Lanreath turning. Look out for the signs. (29 miles from Plymouth city centre)

Tamar Otter Sanctuary: North Petherwin, near Launceston. Tel: (01566) 785646. A branch of the Otter Trust where British otters are bred for release into the wild. Wood with fallow and muntjac deer and lakes with waterfowl. Picnic areas, illustrated nature trail, refreshments. Off the B3254 road to Bude. (31 miles from Plymouth city centre)

Tamar Valley Donkey Park: St. Anns Chapel, near Gunnislake. Tel: (01822) 834072. Donkeys and other tame animals; donkey rides and cart rides; picnic areas; woodland walks; children's play area, café. (17 miles from Plymouth city centre)

Trebah Garden: Mawnan Smith, near Falmouth, TR11 5JZ Tel: (01326) 250448 Trebah is a wonderful garden for families. There are trails for children of all ages to follow round the garden; they are especially amazed by the path through a jungle of giant rhubarb and love to race around The Bamboozle. Enjoy the surprise on their faces as they find themselves on the private beach on the Helford - a perfect place for a swim and a picnic, or just to watch the colourful sailing boats. Trebah also has a wheelchair route and three electric buggies that visitors can borrow. Between Falmouth and Helston off the A394 (68 miles from Plymouth)

Trethorne Leisure Farm: Kennards House, Launceston Tel: (01566) 86324. Climbing wall, slides, ballpools, ten pin bowling, roller blading, gladiator duel, trampolines, assault course, pony rides. (26 miles from Plymouth city centre)

The Yarg Cheese Farm: Netherton Farm, Upton Cross, Liskeard, PL14 5BD. Tel: (01579) 362244. Watch cheese-making with guided tours (cheese-making not always available on Saturdays). Between Launceston and Liskeard on the B3254, approx 6 miles north of Liskeard. Nature trails, picnic site, orchard, woodland walk, tearoom. (25 miles from Plymouth city centre)

BEACHES

These are some of the beaches in the South Devon and South East Cornwall area. SA indicates that they have been given a Seaside Award (2003) by the Tidy Britain Group. To view all the beaches with a Seaside Award go to www.parents-guide-to-plymouth.co.uk/beaches.htm where predicted tide times can also be accessed.

At **Wembury Beach**, close to the city (accessed via the A379 through Plymstock) the Wembury Marine Centre offers activities throughout the summer holiday. Map reference SX 517 485. See also page 65 (children's activities).

SOUTH DEVON
Bantham: large, fine sand beach with rockpools running from the mouth of the river Avon behind sand dunes. Very popular beach, situated in an area of great natural beauty with views across to Burgh Island. One of the best surfing beaches on the south coast and also popular with windsurfers. At the roundabout on the A379 between Churchstow and Aveton Gifford, follow the signs for Bantham. Café, toilets, dog restricted area. SA

Bigbury-on-Sea: Sandy beach with rock pools, approximately 40 minutes from Plymouth, by car, on the B3392. Toilets, showers, babychange facilities. Award winning beach that is cleaned daily; dogs banned from May to September; café; 900 space car park 75 metres from beach; charges from £2 to £4 per day. SA

Blackpool Sands: very popular coarse sandy beach set in an unspoilt sheltered bay in the South Hams.
Freshwater paddling pond for youngsters. Parking, shop, toilets, showers, café, picnic tables; dogs not permitted. SA

Challaborough: horse-shoe shaped cove with sandy, sheltered beach. Rock pools at low tide. From the A379 between Modbury and Aveton Gifford, turn onto the B3392 towards Bigbury. At St Anns Chapel turn right. signposted Ringmore and Challaborough. Car park with charge. SA

Hope Cove: This is a popular family beach which is sheltered, relatively safe and sandy. Hope Cove is signposted off the A381 between Kingsbridge and Salcombe. Café, toilets. SA

Slapton Sands: The small village of Torcross is at the southern end of the long shingle expanse of Slapton Sands. Behind the beach is the Freshwater Ley, which boasts a host of wildfowl. Torcross is on the A379, Dartmouth Kingsbridge Road. Toilets, car park with charge. SA

South Milton Sands and Thurlestone: Owned by the National Trust and is an area of Outstanding Natural Beauty. A coarse sand beach with rocky outcrops and rockpools at low tide. On the A381 between West Alvington and Marlborough, turn at the signpost to South Milton. Turn left at the Post Office. Car park, café, toilets. SA

Wembury Beach: This is a sandy cove with rock pools and backed by low cliffs. Recommended by the Good Beach Guide 2003 as the finest beach in the Plymouth area, despite the presence of a sewage pipe which prompts the warning to take care when swimming after heavy rain.

SOUTH EAST CORNWALL
Whitsand Bay: Gently curving bay with nearly four miles of sands. The beach is accessed by cliff paths at Freathy with various parking places

along the cliff tops. No easy access for young children or buggies. Dangerous currents in this area.

Cawsand and Kingsand: Narrow streeted villages. Sheltered small sand and shingle beaches. Easy access with all facilities nearby. Safe bathing except on SE winds; dog ban.

Downderry: South facing, fine shingle beach which is sheltered by a sea wall. Rock pools at low tide. Easy access.

Looe beach & Plaidy: Popular sandy beaches with all facilities nearby. Car parking at either the quayside or the main car parks.

Millendreath: A small sheltered beach of sand and fine shingle. The east end of the beach has an artificial tidal swimming pool. Rock pools. Indoor swimming pool in vicinity. Car park, toilets, café.

FURTHER INFORMATION

Information on tourist attractions, accommodation, places to eat, events, etc can be found at the following locations, and on the Plymouth Marketing Bureau website at **www.visitplymouth.co.uk**. Information about local events may also be found in the Evening Herald, Western Morning News, Sunday Independent, Tavistock Times and South Hams and South East Cornwall newspapers, BBC Radio Devon, BBC Radio Cornwall, Pirate FM Radio and Plymouth Sound Radio as well as the local TV Stations.

On the Internet, go to a mapping website, such as www.multimap.com, insert a postcode or place name to check out the location and find a route.

Plymouth Tourist Information Centre: Island House, 9 The Barbican, Plymouth, PL1 2LS. Tel: (01752) 304849

Plymouth Tourist Information Centre: Crabtree (Marsh Mills Roundabout), Plymouth, PL3 6RN. Tel: (01752) 266030/266031

Dartmoor High Moorland Visitor Centre: Duchy Building, Tavistock Road, Princetown. Tel: (01822) 890414 (open throughout the year)

Ivybridge (South Dartmoor) Tourist Information Centre: Leonards Road, Ivybridge, PL21 0SL. Tel: (01752) 897035

Tavistock Tourist Information Centre: Town Hall, Bedford Square, Tavistock, PL19 0AE. Tel: (01822) 612938

PARKS AND PLAYGROUNDS

Within the Plymouth city boundary there are many designated parks, including the following:

Central Park, Milehouse/Peverell - the largest park in Plymouth and now with an exciting new play area on the theme of 7 continents with a range of wet and dry facilities, suitable for children with disabilities.

A new youth park is planned for Spring 2004, to include Skate Board facilities, multi-sports wall, performance area and sheltered seating.

Astor Park, off the Cattedown roundabout

Beaumont Park, St Judes
Chaddlewood Park, Plympton
Devonport Park, Devonport
Freedom Park, Lipson
Hartley Park, Higher Compton
Oreston Play Park, Oreston
Pounds Park, Peverell
Thorn Park, Mannamead
Tothill Park, St Judes
Victoria Park, Millbridge
West Hoe Park, West Hoe (See also p 20)

There are approximately 160 children's playgrounds in the city, and the Parks Services have an on-going programme of improvements. A number of them now have new equipment and safety surfaces and some have dog-proof fencing. For further information contact the City Parks Services on (01752) 606034.

PUBS AND RESTAURANTS IN THE PLYMOUTH AREA WHICH WELCOME CHILDREN

The following establishments have provided information regarding their facilities. There are no doubt many other places that welcome families and the author would like to obtain feedback from families on their favourite places. Please get in touch by post or email, with details of family-friendly establishments for inclusion in the next edition.

Key:

H – high chairs	N – nappy changing facilities
B – heating babies' bottles	NU – unisex facilities
V – vegetarian meals	Party – organise children's parties
P – children's portions	NS – non-smoking restaurant
M – children's menu	NS area – section for non-smokers
Vegan – vegan meals	F – family area (in a pub)
BM – welcome breastfeeding mums	PI – play area indoors
	PO – play area outdoors

Currently children should leave licensed premises by 9.00 pm. This is changing to midnight if accompanied by an adult, from 2005.

Many places are happy to welcome breast-feeding mothers provided they are discreet. A number that are marked "Vegan" do not have a vegan menu but are able and willing to provide appropriate meals.

PLYMOUTH:

Athenian Restaurant, 111 Mayflower Street. Tel: (01752) 266932. Cater for children: 11.30 am – 2.00 pm, 5.00 – 11.00 pm. H,B,V,P, M,Vegan,BM,Party.

BHS, 33/39 Cornwall Street, PL1 1NR. Tel: (01752) 667640 Opening hours: 9.00 am – 5.30 pm Mon – Thurs, 8.30 am – 6.00 pm Sat, 10.00 am – 4.00 pm Sun H,B,V,P,M,BM,NU,NS area

The Brasserie, Mayflower Marina, Richmond Walk. Tel: (01752) 500008 Opening hours: 11.00 am – 3.00 pm, 7.00 pm – 11.00 pm H,B, V,P,Vegan, BM,N

Burger King, 34 Cornwall Street, PL1 1LP. Tel: (01752) 265752. Opening hours: 8.00 am – 8.00 pm. H,B,V,M,BM,F.

Burger King, 97 New George Street, PL1 1RQ. Tel: (01752) 228914. Opening hours: 8.30 am – 11.00 pm. H,B,V,M,BM,NU,F.

The Café, Unit 7, Eastlake Walk. Tel: (01752) 252656 Opening Hours: 10.00 am – 4.00 pm. H,B,V,P,M,BM,NU,NS,Pl. The Café has a play barn for 2 to 7 year olds at £1.50 per hour and the children are given a free squash. There is a soft play area which is free to under 2 year olds.

Café Rouge, 11 Whimple Street, St Andrews Cross. Tel: (01752) 665522. Cater for children: 10.00 am – 11.00 pm. H,B,V,P,M,Vegan,BM,NU, Party,NS area.

Captain Jaspers,The Whitehouse Pier, Barbican, PL1 2LS An outdoor eating experience down on the quay. Opening hours: Mon – Sat 7.30 am – 11.45 pm, Sun 8.00 am – 11.45 pm B,V,P,Vegan,BM

Debenhams, Royal Parade, PL1 1LA. Tel: (01752) 266666 Opening hours: 9.30 am – 6.00 pm Mon – Wed; 9.30 am – 7.00 pm Thur; 9.00 am – 6.00 pm Fri & Sat; 11.00 am – 5.00 pm Sun. H,B,V,P,M, BM, NU, NS

Derrys, Co-operative House, Derry's Cross. Tel: (01752) 303030. Opening hours: 9.00 am – 5.00 pm Mon,Tues,Wed, 9.00 am – 6.00 pm Thurs, 9.00 am – 5.30 pm Fri,Sat, 10.30 am – 4.00 pm Sun H,B,V,P,Vegan,M,BM,NU,Party,NS area.

DIngles, Royal Parade. Tel: (01752) 266611 Opening hours: 9.00 am – 5.30 pm Mon, Wed; 9.30 am – 5.30 pm Tue; 9.00 am – 7.00 pm Thur; 9.00 am – 6.00 pm Sat. H,B,V,P,M,BM,NU,Pl.

Duke of Cornwall Hotel, Millbay Road. Tel: (01752) 275850. Cater for children: 7.00 pm – 10.00 pm. H,B,V,P,Vegan,BM,NU,Party,NS.

Dutton's Café Continental, Madeira Road, The Hoe. Tel: (01752) 255245 Opening hours: 10.00 am – 5.00 pm (closed Wednesdays) H,B,V,P,M,Vegan,BM, NS, PO

The Eddystone Inn, Heybrook Bay, Nr Plymouth, PL9 0BN. Tel: (01752) 862356. Cater for children: 11.30 am – 2.30 pm, 6.30 pm – 9.00 pm H,B,V,P,M,NS.

Elliott's Brasserie, Plymouth Moat House, Armada Way. Tel: (01752)

```
THE MUSSEL INN
Down Thomas, Plymouth
PL9 0AQ
(01752) 862238

******

A warm welcome and great
food for the whole family

Children's outdoor play area

Children's & vegetarian menus

A la carte menu

Large car park
```

639937 Cater for children: 9.00 am – 7.00 pm H,B,V,P,M, Vegan,BM,NU,Party,NS,Pl **George Hotel**, 399 Tavistock Road, Roborough. Tel: (01752) 771527 Food available: 12.00 – 9.00 pm Sun to Thur; 12.00 – 10.00 pm Fri & Sat. H,B,V,P,M,BM,NU,NS area,F,Pl.Children's play area open from 12.00 noon – 8.00 pm Sun to Thur and 12.00 – 9.00 pm Fri & Sat. **Harbour Seafood and Pasta Restaurant**, 10 Quay Road, The Barbican. Tel: (01752) 260717. Cater for children: 11.30 am – 8.00 pm. H,B,V,P,BM,NU,NS area. **Hobbs Coffee and Chocolate House**, 29-31 Eastlake Street, PL1 1BU. Tel: (01752) 267541. Cater for children: 7.30 am – 5.00 pm Mon to Sat; 10.00 am – 4.00 pm Sun. H,B,V,P,BM,NS area.

Kentucky Fried Chicken have premises at the following locations in Plymouth:
116 New George Street, PL1 1RZ, 27 Tavistock Road, Crownhill, Mutley Plain, St Budeaux. Cater for children: 11.00 am – 11.00 pm. H,P,M,BM,N, NS.

Kings Arms, 15 The Quay, Oreston, PL9 7NE. Tel: (01752) 401277 H,B,V,P,M,Vegan,BM, NS area.

Lanterns Kebab and Steak House, 88 Cornwall Street, PL1 1LR. Tel: (01752) 665516. Cater for children: 11.30 am – 11.00 pm. H,B,V,P,M, Vegan,BM,N,Party,NS area.

Leandra Restaurant, 19 Frankfort Gate. Tel: (01752) 266176. Cater for children: 11.30 am – 10.30 pm. H,B,V,P,M,Vegan,BM,NS area.

Les Jardins de Bagatelle, 11 Old Town Street. Tel: (01752) 257786. Opening hours: 7.30 am – 6.30 pm. B,V,BM,N,NS.

The Lockyers Quay, 1 Lockyers Quay, Coxside. Tel: (01752) 254180. Cater for children: 11.00 am – 10.00 pm H,B,V,P,M,Vegan,BM,NU, NS area,PO

The Lopes Arms, Roborough, PL6 7BD. Tel: (01752) 301411. Cater for children: 11.00 am – 8.00 pm. H,B,V,Vegan,P,M,BM,NS area.

The Lord Louis, Glen Road, Plympton, PL7 2DE. Tel: (01752) 339562 Cater for children: 11.30 am – 9.00 pm H,B,V,P,M,BM,NS,

Lorenzo's, Athenaeum Place, Derry's Cross. Tel: (01752) 201522 Opening hours: 12.00 noon – 12.00 midnight H,B,V,P,M,BM,Party

The Lyneham Inn, Old A38, Plympton, PL7 5AT. Tel: (01752) 336955. Cater for children: 12.00 noon – 2.30 pm; 6.00 – 9.00 pm H,B,V, P,M,Vegan,BM,NS area, PO.

McDonald's Restaurant, 13 New George Street. Tel: (01752) 255030 Opening hours: 7.00 am – 11.00 pm Sun to Thurs; 7.00 am – 12.00 midnight Fri and Sat. H,B,V,P,M,BM,NU,Party,NS,PI.

McDonald's Restaurant, Pomphlett Road. Tel: (01752) 484137 Opening hours: 7.00 am – 11.00 pm. H,B,V,P,M,NU,Party,NS.

There are also McDonald's Restaurants at Barbican Leisure Park, Coypool Road, Plympton, Tavistock Road, Crownhill and 100 New George Street, Plymouth.

Marsh Mills Beefeater, 300 Plymouth Road, Crabtree. Tel: (01752) 600660. Cater for children: 7.00 am – 9.00 pm. H,B,V,P,M,Vegan, BM,NU,NS,PO .

Miners Arms, Hemerdon, Plympton, PL7 5BU. Tel: (01752) 336040. Cater for children: 11.00 am – 2.30 pm; 5.30 – 9.00 pm Mon to Thur; all day Fri to Sun. H,B,V,P,M, Vegan,BM,N,NS,PI,PO.

The Mussel Inn, Down Thomas, Plymouth, PL9 0AQ Tel: (01752) 862238 Cater for children: 12.00 – 2.00 pm and 6.45 – 9.00 pm (9.30 pm at weekends) H,B,V,P,M,Vegan,BM,NS area,F,PI,PO

Novotel Hotel, 270 Plymouth Road, Plympton. Tel: (01752) 221422. Cater for children: 6.00 am – 12.00 midnight. H,B,V,P,M,Vegan, BM,NU,Party,NS area,PI,PO.

O'Brien's Sandwich Bar, 1 Old Town Street, PL1 1DA Tel: (01752) 256441. Opening hours: 7.00 am – 4.45 pm. H,B,V,P,M,Vegan,BM, NU,NS.

Old Orleans, Barbican Leisure Park, Warner Village, Coxside. Tel: (01752) 256470. Cater for children: 12 noon – 11.00 pm. H,B,V,P,M,Vegan, BM,NU,NS area,

Pasta and Pizza Bar, 9 Market Avenue, PL1 1PE. Tel: (01752) 266336. Cater for children: 11.30 am – 11.00 pm. H,B,V,P,BM,Party

Pasta Bar on the Barbican, 40 Southside Street, Barbican, PL1 2LE. Tel: (01752) 671299. Cater for children: 11.30 am – 11.00 pm. H,B,V,P,BM,NS area,Party

Pizzaghetti, 23 Southside Street, Barbican, PL1 2LD. Tel: (01752) 665345. Cater for children: 11.30 am – 2.30 pm; 5.30 – 11.00 pm . Open all day Fri and Sat. B,V,P,M,BM.

Pizza Hut, Barbican Leisure Park, Coxside. Tel: (01752) 255881 Opening hours: 11.30 am – 11.00 pm. H,B,V,P,M,Vegan,BM,N, Party,NS,PI.

Pizza Hut, 76-78 Royal Parade, PL1 1EW Tel: (01752) 254625 Opening hours: 11.30 am – 11.00 pm. H,B,V,P,M,Vegan,BM,N, Party,NS,PI.

The HUNTING LODGE
Cadleigh Park, nr Ivybridge on the A38
Tel: (01752) 892409

Freshly Prepared Cuisine
Children's and Vegetarian Menus
Fine Quality at Realistic Prices

FOXES DEN: a fun play area for youngsters to climb, play & explore

Pizza Hut, Tavistock Road, Crownhill. Tel: (01752) 709800 Opening hours: 11.30 am – 10.30 pm Sun to Thurs; 11.30 am – 11.00 pm Fri & Sat. H,B,V,P,M,BM,NU,Party,NS,F.
Platters, 12 The Barbican, PL1 2LS. Tel: (01752) 227262. Cater for children: 11.30 am – 10.30 pm. H,B,V,P,M,Vegan,BM
Plymouth Arts Centre, Looe Street, Bretonside. Tel: (01752) 206114. Cater for children: 12.00 – 2.00 pm, 5.00 – 8.30 pm. (Not open Sunday; Monday only 12.00 – 2.00 pm). H,B,V,Vegan, BM,NS area.
Porters, 20-21 Looe Street, Bretonside, PL4 0EA. Cater for children: 12.00 noon – 3.00 pm. B,V,BM, Beer garden.
Positano Restaurant, 36-38 Mayflower Street, PL1 1QX. Cater for children: 12.00 noon – 1.30 pm, 6.00 pm – 10.00 pm. B,V,P,BM,NU.
Rising Sun Inn, 138 Eggbuckland Road. Tel: (01752) 774359. Cater for children: 12.00 noon – 9.00 pm. B,V,P,M,NU.
Ship's Tavern, Arcadia Road, Elburton. Tel: (01752) 401626 Cater for children: 12.00 noon – 2.00 pm; 6.00 pm – 9.00 pm. H,B,V, P, M, NS.
Sir Joshua Reynolds, The Ridgeway, Plympton. Tel: (01752) 336982. Cater for children: 11.30 am – 2.00 pm, 6.30 – 8.30 pm. H,B,V,P,M, Vegan,BM,NS.
The Tap and Barrel, Ashford Crescent, Mutley. Tel: (01752) 663603. Cater for children: 11.00 am – 9.00 pm. H,B,V,M,BM,N,Party,F.
The Unicorn, Plymouth Road, Plympton. Tel: (01752) 337939. Cater for children: 11.00 am – 9.00 pm. H,B,V,M,BM,NU,Party,NS area,F, PI,PO.
Offer a Deep Sea Den play area with an hourly charge.
Union Inn, 17 Underwood Road, Plympton. Tel: (01752) 337294. Cater for children: 11.30 am – 2.30 pm, 5.00 – 9.00 pm. B,V,P,BM,F,PO.
Village Restaurant, 32 Southside Street, Barbican. Tel: (01752) 667688. Cater for children: 11.30 am – 2.00 pm, 5.30 – 9.00 pm. B,V,P,M,Vegan,BM,NU.
Wimpy Restaurant, 22 Cornwall Street, PL1 1LR. Tel: (01752) 225090. Cater for children: 9.00 am – 8.15 pm. H,V,P,M,BM,N,Party,PI.
Zeus, 150 Cornwall Street. Tel: (01752) 661843. Cater for children: 11.00 am – 11.00 pm. H,B,V,P,M, Vegan.
CORNWALL:
The Crooked Inn, Stoketon Cross, Saltash, PL12 4RZ Tel: (01752) 848177 Cater for children 12.00 noon – 2.30 pm Mon to Sat, 12.00 – 3.00 Sun, 6.00 pm – 930 pm Sun to Thur, 6.00 pm – 10.00 pm Fri & Sat. H,B,V,P,M,BM,N, P, NS area, F,PO

The Holland Inn, Hatt, Saltash, PL12 6PJ Tel: (01752) 844044 Opening hours: 11.00 am – 11.00 pm H,B,V,P,M,Vegan,BM,NU,Party,NS,F ,PI,PO **Bouncy ball pool, soft play and slide indoors, slide, swings, etc outdoors.**
Who'd Have Thought It Inn, St Dominick, Saltash. Tel: (01579) 350214. Cater for children: 11.30 am – 2.30 pm; 6.30 – 9.00 pm. H,B,V,P,M,BM,NS area.

DEVON:
The Burrator Inn, Dousland, Yelverton. Tel: (01822) 853121. Cater for children: 11.00 am – 9.00 pm. H,B,V,P,M,BM,NU,Party,NS,F,PO.

The Crooked Spire, Ermington, PL21 9LP Tel: (01548) 831288 Cater for children: 12.00 – 3.00 pm Tues to Sun; 6.00 – 9.00 pm Mon to Sun; H,B,V,P,M,BM,N,Party,NS

The Elephant's Nest Inn, Horndon, Peter Tavy, near Tavistock Tel: (01822) 810273 Cater for children: 12.00 noon – 3.00 pm and 6.30 – 9.00 pm B,V,P,M,Vegan,NS area, F. Large, safe garden.

The Holland Inn
Hotel
Callington Road, Hatt, Saltash
(01752) 844044
FUN FOR ALL THE FAMILY
Indoor & Outdoor play area
Children's parties
skittle alley here too!

The Hunting Lodge, Cadleigh Park, near Ivybridge, PL21 9JN Tel: (01752) 892409 Cater for children: 12.00 noon – 9.00 pm. H,B,V,P,M, Vegan, BM, NU,Party,NS,F,PI. **Foxes Den Play Area has pool ball, slides, ramps £1.25 entry with no time limit.**
Mary Tavy Inn, Lane Head, Mary Tavy, Tavistock. Tel: (01822) 810326 Cater for children: 11.45 am – 2.30 pm Wed to Sun; 6.30 – 9.00 pm Mon to Sun. H,B,V,P,M,Vegan,BM,NS
The Mildmay Colours, Fore Street, Holbeton. Tel: (01752) 830248 Cater for children: 11.00 am – 3.00 pm, 6.00 – 9.00 pm H,B,V,P,M,BM,NS,F,PO
The Pickwick Inn, St Ann's Chapel, Bigbury on Sea Tel: (01548) 810241 Cater for children: 11.00 am – 9.00 pm H,B,V,P,M,Vegan,BM,NU, P,NS,F,PO
The White Thorn Inn, Shaugh Prior, near Plymouth. Tel: (01752) 839245. Cater for children: 11.00 am – 3.00 pm, 6.00 – 9.00 pm. H,B,V,P,M,BM,N, Party,PO. **Play area with slide, climbing frame, wendy house.**

CINEMAS AND THEATRES

The following venues are likely to offer special shows and productions for children at Christmas and in the holiday periods.

ABC Cinema, Derrys Cross, Plymouth. Tel: (01752) 663300 (Enquiries), (01752) 255655 (Advance Booking Line).

Barbican Theatre: Castle Street, Barbican, Plymouth PL1 2NJ. Tel: (01752) 267131 Visit the website at www.barbicantheatre.co.uk

Plymouth Arts Centre Cinema: 38 Looe Street, Plymouth. Tel: (01752) 206114

Plymouth Athenaeum Theatre: Derrys Cross, Plymouth. Tel: (01752) 266104

Plymouth Pavilions: Millbay Road, Plymouth. Tel: (01752) 229922 (Box office). Membership of Pavilions PALs allows priority booking for most shows, information on activities sent out regularly, discounts on sporting activities. Tel. (01752) 222200 for an application form. Check out the Website at www.plymouthpavilions.com

Theatre Royal and Drum Theatre: Royal Parade, Plymouth PL1 2TR. Tel: (01752) 267222 (Box office) Membership of the Mailing Club or TRAC allows priority booking for most shows, information on productions sent out regularly. Visit the website at www.theatreroyal.com

Warner Village Cinemas: Barbican Leisure Park, Barbican Approach, Coxside, Plymouth. Tel: 08702 406020 (24 hour Bookings and Information Line)

To find out which films are showing in your area visit the website at www.parents-guide-to-plymouth.co.uk/cinemas.htm and follow the link to a site that also includes reviews of current films.

TRANSPORT FACILITIES IN AND AROUND PLYMOUTH

Traveline is a "one-stop" shop for public transport timetables. It is a database of rail, bus and coach times throughout the South West, which uses global positioning technology. Call 0870 6082 608 (national rate) to be put through to the local centre where an operator will have access to all the latest rail, bus and coach timetables and can map out a tailor-made journey. Further information on travel services can also be found at the Tourist Information Centres (see page 36).

IT terminals have been established through the Local Transport Plan. They provide free up-to-the minute transport information at the push of a button through public information terminals and give access to bus, train and ferry timetables across Devon and Cornwall together with national coach and rail services. The terminals are in Royal Parade, the Civic Centre, Plymouth Barbican and St Budeaux square.

First Great Western produce a leaflet entitled "Transport Links - A Guide to transport links in South Devon and Cornwall" giving details of linked rail and bus services throughout the area, available at Plymouth Railway Station.

AIR TRAVEL
Air Southwest operate flights from Plymouth Airport at Roborough (in the north of the city) and Newquay Airport in Cornwall to London Gatwick. From 1st March 2004 they will offer flights to Manchester and Bristol. Tel: 0870 241 8202

Air Wales fly from Plymouth Airport to Cork and Dublin in Ireland, Jersey in the Channel Islands (summer only), as well Cardiff, Newcastle and Liverpool. Children under 2 travel free; accompanied children under 16 years travel at half-price. For further information tel: 0870 777 3131.

Refreshments are available at the airport until the last flight leaves. There are no separate facilities for nursing mothers; a changing mat is provided in the ladies' toilet. For further information tel: (01752) 204090

BOAT
A cross-Channel car ferry service from Plymouth to Roscoff in Brittany and Santander in Spain is operated by Brittany Ferries. Children under four years of age travel free. Special fares for children aged between four and fifteen years. Refreshments available to coincide with ferry arrivals and departures. There is a nappy changing cubicle in the terminal. Millbay Docks, Millbay Road, Plymouth. For reservations Tel: 08705 360 360

The **Cremyll Pedestrian Ferry** operates from Admiral's Hard (off Durnford Street, Stonehouse) to Mount Edgcumbe Park. A ferry timetable may be purchased at the Cremyll Tollgate. Telephone enquiries about the ferry can be made on (01752) 822105.

The **Mount Batten Ferry** (water taxis) operates daily between the Barbican and Mount Batten. Tel: 07930 838614 or (01752) 408590

Plymouth Boat Cruises operate boat trips from Plymouth Barbican, also linking with the Tamar Valley Line trains. For further information tel: (01752) 822797.

Tamar Passenger Ferry travels between Calstock, Bere Alston and Cotehele Quay during the summer, depending on the tides. For further information tel: (01822) 833331.

The **Torpoint Ferry** is a regular and frequent car and pedestrian ferry service operating between Torpoint and Devonport. Telephone enquiries can be made on (01752) 812233.

BUS
Plymouth Citybus: Milehouse, Plymouth. Tel: (01752) 222221 (Information hotline). Up to 3 accompanied children under five years of

age travel free on all services. Children aged 5 to 15 travel at around half the adult fare at off peak times. All children of secondary school age should carry a "Young Person's Travel Pass" to show entitlement to reductions and the purchase of Scholars' Season Tickets. All fares are charged according to the distance travelled, with day returns being available after 0900 Monday to Friday, and all day Saturday, Sunday and Bank Holidays. There are various discount tickets, including half termly StudentRiders and SchoolRiders for term time journeys, and an off-peak FamilyRider at £5.50 for one day's travel on Citybus services in Plymouth. Citybus run an extensive network of wheelchair and buggy accessible SuperRider buses on main routes. Information on these and all timetables is available from the Travel Shop (Exeter Street), or by phoning (01752) 222221 from 0800 to 1730 Monday to Friday, and 0900 to 1230 Saturday. Lost Property queries are also on this number, and the property can be collected 0800 to 1700 Monday to Friday from the Milehouse Office. **First**: The Ride, Chelson Meadow, Plymouth, PL9 7JT. Tel: (01752) 402060 Monday to Friday 0800 to 1700 and Saturday 0800 to 1430. City and County Commutacards are available for one month, three months or school term allowing discount travel. Lost property queries can be made on (01752) 254542 between 0830 to 1800 Monday to Saturday and 0900 to 1700 Sunday.

Information on School Travel passes can be found at www.parents-guide-to-plymouth.co.uk/transpor.htm

CAR SHARING

Go to www.parents-guide-to-plymouth.co.uk/transpor.htm on the Internet, for details of Devon County car sharing scheme. This aims to match people wanting lifts with those travelling in the same direction.

CYCLING

There are cycle paths at various points through the city and recreational cycle ways (eg in the Plym Valley). Leaflets detailing these routes can be obtained from the Plymouth Tourist Information Centres.

For information on cycling in Plymouth or for a copy of the Plymouth Cycle Guide please contact the Transport & Planning Service, Road Safety Team, Plymouth City Council, Civic Centre, Floor 10, Plymouth, PL1 2EW, Tel (01752) 307730 or email roadsafety@plymouth.gov.uk. Copies of the guide are also available from most bike shops, libraries and tourist information centres in Plymouth.

TRAIN

The Plus Bus website, www.plusbus.org.uk explains all about The Plus Bus scheme which entitles ticket holders to unlimited travel on a network of buses within a specified area around Plymouth. It works by adding a small charge to the train fare, involving the use of just one ticket.

First Great Western offer their Family Carriage (Coach E) on most off-peak services during school holidays and Saturdays and Sundays. They give free activity packs for children at the buffet. There are babychange facilities and seats with storage space for buggies. Children under five travel free. To book tel: 08457 000 125. For up-to-date information on train times and fares tel: 08457 484950.

Wessex Trains operate a network of services throughout the westcountry, including main line and branch line services. Locally Wessex trains run services on the scenic Tamar Valley Line, which links Plymouth to the Bere Peninsula, Calstock and Gunnislake, through the Tamar Valley's Area of Outstanding Natural Beauty. The Tamar Valley is a wonderful place to walk with a number of village, riverside and woodland trails to be enjoyed. The National Trust Property of Cotehele is a pleasant mile and a half walk from Calstock but can also be accessed by passenger ferry from Calstock Quayside (seasonal operation Tel: (01822) 833331). Details of local walking routes are available from local Tourist Information Centres or from the Devon and Cornwall Rail Partnership (01752) 233094.

Dartmoor Sunday Rover: Tamar Valley Sunday Services link, year round, to a network of bus routes that cross Dartmoor. In the summer the network is extended and includes the Okehampton-Exeter Dartmoor Railway. Enjoy unlimited travel on this network of Sunday services with a Sunday Rover Ticket. Pick up the Sunday Rover leaflet at local manned stations, Tourist information Centres or by calling (01392) 32800 or (01752) 233094 (office hours).

The **Devon & Cornwall Rail Partnership** produce a series of leaflets including Line Guides and Timetables giving information on branch lines throughout Devon & Cornwall; for further information visit www.carfreedaysout.com.

For information on all train times and services, local and national, contact National Rail Enquiries on 08457 48 49 50.

SHOPMOBILITY
Plymouth Shopmobility and Community Transport provides a range of transport services to help people in the city who have limited mobility. For further information on the areas of the city where there is provision telephone (01752) 600633.

PLYMOUTH LOCAL NATURE RESERVES are areas of land which are set aside by Local Authorities and managed for the benefit of the habitats, animals and plants they contain as well as providing facilities for the quiet enjoyment of nature by the public. Plymouth has six Nature Reserves, designated under the National Parks and Access to the Countryside Act 1949, A leaflet is available for each reserve which shows its location, details of the points of interest on each walk through, and includes drawings of some of the plant and animal life to be found in the area. Copies of the leaflets can be obtained from the Plymouth Tourist Information Centres (see page 36) and the Enquiry Desk in the Civic Centre. Further information may also be obtained by phoning the City Planning Office on (01752) 304229, or visiting the Internet at www.parents-guide-to-plymouth.co.uk/plymlnr.htm

COUNTRY CODE

You can help your children to grow up with a respect for the countryside by ensuring that they understand and adhere to the following Country Code prepared by the National Parks Commission.

- Guard against all risk of fire
- Keep dogs under proper control
- Keep to paths across farmland
- Leave no litter
- Safeguard water supplies
- Protect wildlife, wild plants and trees
- Go carefully on country roads
- Avoid making unnecessary noise
- Respect the life of the countryside

EDUCATION, DAY CARE AND LEISURE

CHILDCARE

The Government-funded **Plymouth Children's Information Service**, located in Marlborough Street, Devonport, keeps details of all of the Ofsted registered provision in the Plymouth area:

- Childcare Information
- Childminders
- Creches
- Pre-school/Playgroups
- Family Centres
- Holiday Clubs and Playschemes
- Before and after school clubs

Plus the following:

- Family support information
- Parenting classes
- Youth clubs
- Leisure activities
- Childcare job vacancies

By contacting the Plymouth Children's Information Service you can be assured that your childcare provision satisfies current requirements and is properly registered. Please note that there is limited provision for nursery places for very young children. If you need a place for your child from the age of three months, it is very important to get your name down with an appropriate provider as soon as the pregnancy is confirmed.

Details of the local information service and factsheets on childcare options are available from the Plymouth Children's Information Service on freephone 0800 783 4259.

ALL CHILDREN FIRST

The Government's National Childcare Strategy has set ambitious targets for creating high quality, affordable, accessible early years and childcare services throughout the country. All Children First (Plymouth Early Years Development & Childcare Partnership) was developed to implement this strategy in Plymouth, and works closely with the Government's Sure Start Unit and the Local Education Authority (Plymouth City Council).

Representatives from childcare providers and many childcare and early years organisations are included on this partnership and attend regular meetings. By keeping their membership, working practices and progress under review, All Children First ensure that they engage as many different sectors of the community as possible so that childcare is available across Plymouth to meet the needs of all parents.

All Children First is:
• Helping to plan and develop good quality, sustainable childcare and early years services for children aged 0 – 14 years (16 for special educational needs) in Plymouth, and making them affordable and accessible to all.
• Encouraging the recruitment of new workers in to the childcare and early years sectors
• Training existing and new workers to a high standard
• Providing information for parents on Ofsted registered childcare and early years services in the city
• Providing information for, and assisting those wishing to provide childcare and early years services in Plymouth

For more information about All Children First please contact the Early Years Team on (01752) 307 450. Other information is available at www.plymouth.gov.uk/allchildrenfirst

Plymouth Inclusion Childcare Support Service (PICSS)
PICSS is funded by All Children First through the Department for Lifelong Learning to support inclusive childcare for children and young people with special needs from birth to 16 years. Settings are able to have use of a well-equipped resource base as well as support, advice and training. The "Inclusion Works" project, funded by the Children's Fund supports children and young people with special educational needs aged 5 to 13 years in holiday play schemes. PICSS is based at the Jan Cutting Healthy Living Centre, Scott Business Park, Beacon Park Road, Plymouth, PL2 2PQ. Tel: (01752) 314338.

The Plymouth Local Information System for Parenting
(**www.plymouthlisp.org.uk**) has an extensive database of information, relating to services which offer information, education and support for parenting. This database is currently held by the Plymouth Parent Partnership Service, Martins Gate, Bretonside, Plymouth, PL4 0AT. Tel: (01752) 258933.

The Beckly Centre

Mayers Way, Hooe Road, Plymstock, Plymouth PL9 9DF. Tel: (01752) 484433. The Beckly Centre is a registered charity that provides a range of affordable and accessible leisure time play, social and recreational activities and opportunities for children and young people with disability. The Centre provides term time evening and weekend clubs, short residential breaks and outings and day time playscheme sessions during all school holidays together with longer residential breaks away from Plymouth.

Sessions are open to all children and young people in the Plymouth area with extra specific or special needs and provide centre based arts crafts music play (bouncy castle soft play) games bikes trikes videos TV computer / Internet offering social and play opportunities. There are also trips for bowling cinema and swimming. Where spaces are available these

The Beckly Centre
Mayers Way, Hooe Road, Plymstock,
Plymouth, PL9 9DF Tel: (01752) 484433

Play, social, recreational, sports, respite and leisure activities and opportunities provided throughout the year, for children and young people with disability/specific needs who require special care, support and attention.

are open to siblings, friends and family members

Groups are divided by ability/age (min 4 1/2 years to young adult)/ development stage. Wheelchair facilities available including hoist. A wide range of disabilities can be catered for, both physical and learning disability, excluding nursing needs. Limited transport service is available by minibus with tail lift conversion. For further information go to www.parents-guide-to-plymouth.co.uk/beckly.htm

NURSERY PROVISION

The Nursery Education Grant is a grant paid to the local education authority to provide a funded part-time place for every three and four year old within the authority. A child is entitled to a place as follows:

If his/her third birthday falls between 1st April and 31st August he/she is entitled to a funded place from the following September

If his/her third birthday falls between 1st September and 31st December he/she is entitled to a funded place from the following January

If his/her third birthday falls between 1st January and 31st March he/she is entitled to a funded place from the following April.

This funding continues until your child starts school. Your child is entitled to a total of five 2 1/2 hour sessions per week free of charge, for up to 11 weeks per term. If your child attends more than a total of five 2 1/2 hour sessions per week you may be required to pay an additional charge.

The funded place may be at a nursery school, primary school with a nursery class or unit, primary school foundation class, private day nursery, pre-school playgroup, family centre, independent school or accredited childminder. The setting you choose must be registered to claim funding and must pass the appopriate inspection by Ofsted (see below). Telephone the Plymouth Children's Information Service on **FREEPHONE 0800 783 4259** for a list of registered providers.

It is best to visit the possible providers to assess their suitability for your child and ensure you register your child by the headcount date (ask your provider for details).

The provider will inform the Local Education Authority that your child is attending and will claim the funding to cover the cost of the place. Nursery schools and classes provide a core day of 9am to 3.30pm.

Children are offered full time and part time places. These vary in different settings. An afternoon or morning session lasts for 2 1/2 hours. The majority of nursery schools offer extended day provision, which is usually from 8am to 6pm and referred to as wraparound care. Most nursery schools open throughout the school year. Nursery schools and classes are part of the Foundation Stage. Through well-planned play, children will develop skills such as speaking, listening, persistence, concentration, learning to work together and co-operate with other children, as well as early reading, writing and numbers. This will give them the best chance of achieving the Early Learning Goals by the end of their first year in primary school and help ensure they experience the best possible start to their education.

The size of the school or class will vary but the number of staff will reflect the number of children who attend. In maintained nursery schools staffing levels are normally of 2 adults to 20 children with one of the adults being a qualified teacher and the other a qualified nursery assistant. The corresponding staffing levels for maintained nursery classes are 2 adults to 26 children. In private nursery schools staffing levels of 2 adults to 20 children are expected if the head is engaged in teaching or 2 adults to 26 children where the head is excluded. In either case one must be a qualified teacher and the other a qualified nursery assistant.

Funded nursery education settings in the private, voluntary and independent sectors are inspected by Ofsted (Office for Standards in Education). The Plymouth Children's Information Service keeps details of the Plymouth city nursery provision. Links to their Ofsted reports can be found at www.parents-guide-to-plymouth.co.uk/childcar.htm

SUNBEAMS

Sunbeams Day Nursery (Plymouth) Ltd

EDUCATION & CHILDCARE
in a happy homely atmosphere
for children 3 months to 5 years
7.30 am to 6.00 pm 52 weeks
Fully Qualified Experienced Staff
74 Peverell Park Road, Plymouth
Tel: 01752 661445 Fax: 269294

The Nursery Education and Grant Maintained Schools Act 1996 gives the Secretary of State for Education and Skills powers to make grants for nursery education. Section 122 of the Schools Standards and Framework Act 1998 requires Her Majesty's Chief Inspector to arrange the inspection of all nursery settings in the private, voluntary and independent sectors receiving nursery education grant for three- and four-year-olds.

Since October 1996, Registered Nursery Education Inspectors, trained and registered by Ofsted, have been inspecting such settings. Ofsted suggest you contact the Early Years Section at the LEA to confirm whether

a nursery setting is registered to receive grant as part of its Early Years Development and Childcare Plan. Plymouth Early Years Team can be contacted on (01752) 307450. If the LEA has registered the setting for grant, Ofsted will normally carry out an inspection within two terms of the setting first beginning to claim grant.

The inspection report is available from the setting within a month of the inspection. Reports are available via the website approximately three months from the date of inspection. You can ask to see the latest inspection report and registration certificate. Links to the Ofsted reports can be found at www.parents-guide-to-plymouth.co.uk/childcar.htm

Ask the Plymouth Children`s Information Service for more information. They will help you find out about your local options and they will also help if you need extra childcare to match your working hours. Telephone **FREEPHONE 0800 783 4259** for a list of registered providers.

CHILDMINDERS
Childminders look after children on domestic premises in the childminder's own home. They are registered and inspected by Ofsted. Childminders can often be flexible about the hours that they work and they should

provide your child with lots of care, fun and learning.
Childminders can make the most of local parks, playgrounds, toy libraries, drop-in groups and community centres. Often children have the chance to make good friends with the other children who go to their childminder. Some childminders are part of a network and have agreed to meet set quality standards, and some may be accredited to offer Early Years Education.

Childminders must be registered before they begin to work with children. This means checks are carried out to make sure they are suitable to care for children. People over 16 years living in the childminder's household are also police checked to make sure they have not carried out any offence against a child. A check on the childminder's home is carried out as well to make sure it is safe and suitable for children. After registration they are regularly inspected to make sure the childminder is continuing to provide a safe and suitable service. You can ask to see a childminder's registration certificate and latest inspection report. It is illegal for an unregistered person to look after children for reward, unless they are a close relative of the child.

Childminders can care for up to six children aged under eight, of whom no more than three must be aged under five, at any one time. Most childminders are registered for three children under five and three children under eight at any one time. Only one child may be under one year, unless an exception is made by Ofsted, twins for example. The childminder's own children are taken into account and included in these numbers. Childminders who work with an assistant may look after larger groups of children. Children can go to a childminder from a few months old right through until they reach secondary school although they are only registered to look after children aged under 8. Childminders may also care for children between 8 and 14, as long as the number of older children looked after does not adversely affect the care provided for children under 8.

Childminders are self employed and so they decide their working hours. Most childminders will provide you with childcare between the hours of 8am and 6pm. Some childminders will work early mornings, evenings and weekends as well. You will need to negotiate hours, terms and conditions with the childminder. Many childminders are happy to provide families with part-time places for children. They often drop children off at school and pick them up. Childminders can also take your child to a playgroup or pre-school as part of the routine.

The Devon Childminding Association is a registered charity funded by the local authorities of Plymouth, Devon and Torbay to provide advice, information and support to both parents and childminders as well as to provide training for childminders. They are happy to deal with any enquiries about childminding on (01752) 202059 or visit the website via www.parents-guide-to-plymouth/childcar.htm

Ask the Plymouth Children's Information Service (CIS) for advice about childminders in your area. Tel: **FREEPHONE 0800 783 4259**

HOME CHILDCARE

A nanny is employed by you to look after your child in your home. Many have nursery nurse training or childcare qualifications, though this is not compulsory. There is no national nanny register, so, unlike other carers, nannies are not inspected by Ofsted, unless they are a nanny share, and so care for children from more than two families. A nanny can live in or come to your home for set days and hours. You are responsible for checking their credentials and conducting interviews. Nanny share makes this choice more affordable. As the nanny's employer, you must pay their tax and national insurance as well as wages. The Inland Revenue can help work out the tax and national insurance divide for nanny shares. Call their employer helpline on 0845 607 0143.

The Caring Services Team at Plymouth College of Further Education: Goschen Centre, Saltash Road, Keyham, Plymouth, PL2 2DP, offer a two year CACHE Diploma in Child Care and Education Course, an internationally recognised qualification for work with young children. It is worth contacting the Course Tutor before the end of June if you are seeking a nanny. The course is also now available over two years part-time for mature students.

PRE-SCHOOL/PLAYGROUPS

Children in pre-schools are usually aged between three and five but often there are places for children from the age of two and a half years. Pre-schools usually open for sessions of around three hours. Children often attend for morning or afternoon sessions. Sometimes there will be two sessions a day five days a week and sometimes the pre-school just opens once or twice a week. Some pre-schools are open all day. Most pre-schools have the same term dates as local schools. Some offer lunch clubs and before and after school care called "wrap-a-round".

Children in funded early years settings work towards achieving the Early Learning Goals. Through well-planned play, children will develop skills such as speaking, listening, persistence, concentration, learning to work together and co-operate with other children. They will also learn about reading and writing and numbers which will prepare them for Key Stage 1.

Pre-schools, also known as playgroups or playschools, are for young children to learn and play in small groups, often close to their homes. They are registered with Ofsted`s Early Years Directorate and inspected. Some pre-schools also provide free early education through the Nursery Education Grant. Pre-school staff work with children and parents often help out. They offer a range of fun activities for children and lots of opportunities to learn.

Registration and inspection of pre-schools is arranged by Ofsted's Early Years Directorate. This means checks are carried out to ensure that the pre-school staff are suitable to look after children. At least half the staff must be trained to work with children. A check on pre-school premises is carried out to make sure the building is safe and suitable for children. Once the pre-school is registered an inspection is carried out regularly to make sure the pre-school is continuing to provide a safe and suitable service.

Pre-School

We are an Ofsted approved Pre-school, situated in the grounds of Plympton St Maurice school.

Open from 8 am to 5.45 pm

Places available for 2 - 10 years

For more information call Sonia on (01752) 343085

We are here for YOU!

There should be a set number of staff to work with the children. It is recommended that there is one member of staff for every eight children aged three to five and one adult for every four children aged two to three. However, there will often be more adults if parents help out. Most pre-schools will provide places for between 10 to 20 children. There should be no more than 26 children in a group but there may be more than one group within the pre-school. You can ask to see the pre-school`s registration and inspection certificate.

Ask the Plymouth Children`s Information Service (CIS) to tell you more about local pre-schools. **FREEPHONE 0800 783 4259**

OUT OF SCHOOL SERVICES

Out of school services are for school-age children to play and learn and have fun in groups. They are usually based in or near schools and more are being set up to help families where parents work.

Out of school services can be registered with Ofsted provided they are caring for children aged under eight years of age for more than two hours a day and more than six days a year. They are run outside school hours by a team of staff, usually called playworkers. Activities should be planned to help children learn, play and relax with their friends. Playworkers will often pick children up from local schools.

There are different types of out of school services, so look around to find one that suits you and your child.

- Breakfast clubs - open in the mornings before school so children can enjoy breakfast there.
- After school clubs - open in the afternoons between about 3.30pm and 6pm.
- Before and After Clubs - open in the mornings and afternoons.
- Holiday playschemes - open during school holidays between about 8.30am and 6pm

In England, out of school services are also sometimes called kids' clubs. Out of school services registered with Ofsted are checked to make sure the staff are suitable to look after children. At least half of them must be trained and there are rules on the ratio of staff to children depending on the ages of the children catered for. A check is also done on the premises of the registered out of school service to ensure it is safe and suitable for children. After the out of school service is registered an annual inspection is carried out to ensure a safe and suitable service is being provided.

Some out of school services do not currently need to be registered, for example, those which only cater for children aged over eight. You can ask if they are registered. Most out of school services provide places for between 10 and 40 children although some are smaller and others are larger and the age range is usually 5 to 11 years. Some services provide places for three and four year olds to fit around nursery or pre-school education. Some services provide places geared for older children aged 10-14, and sometimes children 15 to 16 with special needs.

Out of school services can open before school and care for children after school until about 6 pm. During the school holidays they are likely to be open between 8.30 am and 6 pm. You may need to book regular sessions to make sure a place is available when you need it.
Contact the Plymouth Children's Information Service (CIS) to find out more about the out of school services. **FREEPHONE 0800 783 4259.**

CRECHES
Facilities that provide occasional care for children under eight. They need to be registered when they run for more than 2 hours a day. They are often available at sports centres, training centres and alongside activities at family or community centres.

PARENT AND TODDLER GROUPS
For parents and their children up to 5 years old (or 3 years old where they are run alongside a playgroup). Their aim is to enable parents to meet, chat and make friends in an informal atmosphere while their children play

with the toys and equipment provided. The play is less organised than in playgroups and the parents must stay with their children. For details of local groups contact the Plymouth Children's Information Service on **FREEPHONE 0800 783 4259**, although groups do not need to be registered. Alternatively ask your Health Visitor who may know of local groups.

The **Pre-school Learning Alliance**: exists to promote and support pre-school/ pre-school/playgroups, and has also taken parent and toddler groups under its wing. More than 70 pre-schools, toddler groups and nurseries are Alliance members within Plymouth. They hold open meetings so that there is a sharing of ideas; members are able to purchase publications related to early years at discounted rates (also available to non-members); a monthly members' magazine with issues relevant to parents, pre-school staff and other interested people is distributed. A range of training including level 2 and 3 qualification courses in childcare is also available. Contact Natalie Harrison (Senior Development Worker) Tel: (01752) 319173

Babysitters:
Babysitting Circles: These are self help groups, some of which operate among friends and neighbours in certain streets or areas and others which are run by young wives clubs, churches, National Childbirth Trust support groups etc. Members babysit for each other on a debit and credit system and no money changes hands. For details of your nearest circle ask your neighbours, or your local church, young wives club, health centre or health visitor.

PLYMOUTH SCHOOLS
To enquire about places at Plymouth Schools, please contact the School Admissions Team, Plymouth City Council Local Education Authority. Tel: (01752) 307469

A list of the Plymouth primary, secondary and special schools with links to Ofsted reports can be viewed at www.parents-guide-to-plymouth.co.uk/schools.htm. A list of the schools is also available from the School Admissions Team.

The Local Education Authority states that:

For all community and voluntary controlled primary and infant schools in Plymouth, the admission criteria are (in order of priority):

1. Children living in the school's designated admissions area with sibling (see below) already attending the school at the time of admission, or attending the linked junior school, for admission to an infant school;
2. other children living in the school's designated admissions area;
3. children living outside the school's designated admissions area with a sibling (see below) already attending the school at the time of admission, or attending the linked junior school, for admission to an infant school;
4. other children living outside the school's designated admissions area.

Notes

Sibling: children are siblings if they are a full, half, step, or adoptive brother or sister, or a child living in the same family unit and household.

Tie Breaker: if there has to be a choice between two or more children in the same category as one another, then the nearer to the school the child lives - by the shortest available walking route - the higher the priority.

SPECIAL EDUCATIONAL NEEDS

The special educational needs of the great majority of children should be met effectively within mainstream settings through *Early Years Action* and *Early Years Action Plus* or *School Action* and *School Action Plus*, without the Local Education Authority needing to make a statutory assessment. In a small number of cases the Local Education Authority will need to make a statutory assessment of special educational needs and then consider whether or not to issue a statement.

The assessment of special educational needs should be seen as a partnership between parents, the professionals contributing advice and the Local Education Authority. The parents and child should be closely involved at each stage of the assessment and encouraged to participate wherever possible. The degree to which the child's views and feelings can be taken into account will vary according to their age and ability.

A statement of special educational needs sets out the child's needs and all the special help he or she should have. The proposed statement will be issued to parents with all the advice obtained during the statutory assessment. If parents are not happy with the proposed statements there are a number of opportunities to request meetings for them to raise their concerns.

The statement will be reviewed on a yearly basis to ensure the provision detailed in the statement is meeting the child's needs. Parents will be encouraged to attend the annual review meeting where their comments, along with school staff and other people working with their child, are discussed. If appropriate, their child will have the opportunity to contribute and participate in the meeting.

The Department for Education and Skills has published a booklet "Special Educational Needs (SEN) – A guide for parents and carers" containing information for parents and explaining the assessment procedure. This can be obtained free of charge by telephoning 0845 60 22260. For further information about provision for children with special educational needs see Plymouth Parent Partnership Service on page 61.

Pre-School Advisory Service
A service for pre-school children who are experiencing delays/difficulties in their development. The service offers support in a flexible and sensitive way to meet the individual needs of children – offering advice, devising programmes for children, working with other services, and running courses for parents, settings and statutory agencies. Jan Cutting Healthy Living Centre, Scott Business Park, Beacon Park Road, Plymouth, PL2 2PQ. Tel: (01752) 314369

Plymouth Portage Service
Portage is a home visiting service which helps parents and carers to teach their children who are developmentally delayed or who have learning disabilities. Portage assesses the needs of these pre-school children and then working together with the parents/carers plans an individual education programme that builds on the child's abilities and teaches new skills. Portage aims to help parents/carers continue to gain satisfaction and success in their role as the main influence on their children's development. Contact is by referral or parents/carers may approach the service direct. Jan Cutting Healthy Living Centre, Scott Business Park, Beacon Park Road, Plymouth, PL2 2PQ Tel: (01752) 314369

Plymouth Psychology Service
The Plymouth Psychology service advises staff in schools and other settings, parents/carers and young people, on all aspects of learning and development. Supports school communities in developing approaches to issues such as inclusion, discipline and bullying. Access to the service may be by referral through school or other agencies. The Mannamead Centre, 15 Eggbuckland Road, Mannamead. Tel: (01752) 224962. See also Plymouth Primary Behaviour Support Team on page 86.

Plymouth Advisory Team for Sensory Impairment
A specialist education service to support infants, children and young people with sensory impairment, their carers, nurseries and educational settings. The team also works closely with other education, health and social services professionals and voluntary agencies. The Mannamead Centre, Eggbuckland Road, Mannamead, Plymouth. The telephone numbers for the teams are:

Hearing Impairment Advisers: Telephone/Minicom/Fax: (01752) 251258

Visual Impairment Advisers: As well as advisory teachers, the visual impairment team includes an Access and Inclusion worker. Tel: (01752) 603214.
(See also Chapter 4 for further information on facilities and assistance for children with special needs.)

Plymouth Hospitals School (see page 109)

For further information on any aspect of education, contact the City of Plymouth Education Office Tel: (01752) 307400

Plymouth Parent Partnership Service
Parent Partnership is a statutory service, managed as part of the Plymouth Psychology Service, but maintained to ensure its independence so that parents/carers have confidence in the neutrality of the service. The Service provides information and support to parents/carers who have concerns about their child's education, including children with special educational needs. Parent Partnership has a network of trained volunteers who can provide support at meetings, help with reports, letters and other paperwork. The service provides information about:
• special educational needs
• children of pre-school age
• exclusions from school
• school admissions
• disability living allowance
• Disagreement Resolution Service
• services available to parents
• leaving school and post-16 opportunities
Martins Gate, Bretonside, Plymouth, PL4 0AT Tel: (01752) 258933
E-mail: jane.taylor@plymouth.gov.uk

HOLIDAY CLUBS AND PLAYSCHEMES
Check out your local community centre or contact the following for details of many of the holiday and half-term activities:
Beckly Centre (for children with special needs) Mayers Way, Hooe Road, Plymstock, Plymouth PL9 9DF. Tel: (01752) 484433 The Centre provides

term time evening and weekend clubs, short residential breaks and outings and day time playscheme sessions during all school holidays together with longer residential breaks away from Plymouth. (see page 50 for further information)

Buckland Abbey, (National Trust), Yelverton, Devon, PL20 6EY Tel: (01822) 853607

Libraries (see "Libraries and Resource Centres" – page 77)

Marjon Sport and Leisure, Derriford Road, Plymouth, PL6 8BH Tel. (01752) 636876

Mayflower Leisure Centre Tel: (01752) 564564

National Marine Aquarium, Rope Walk, Coxside, Plymouth, PL4 0LF. Tel: (01752) 600301.

Plymouth Argyle Community Soccer Club Tel: (01752) 562561.

Plymouth City Council Sports Development Unit Tel: (01752) 307008

Plymouth City Museum and Art Gallery, Drake Circus, Plymouth Tel: (01752) 304779 Offer a range of workshops for children of all ages, usually morning sessions, also some all day; also run term-time events. Phone to receive free mailings of activities.

Plymouth Multi-purpose Sports Centres (see page 74)

Plymouth Outdoor Education Centre, The Mount Batten Centre, 70 Lawrence Road, Plymouth. Tel: (01752) 406444

Plymouth Pavilions, Millbay Road, Plymouth. Tel: (01752) 229922

YMCA Kitto Centre, Honicknowle Lane, Plymouth. Tel: (01752) 201918. To be put on the mailing list to receive regular information on playschemes in the city tel: Freephone 0800 783 4259 (Children's Information Service) as they keep up-to-date information on activities offered by many other providers throughout the city. Go to www.parents-guide-to-plymouth.co.uk/holacts.htm for a current listing of many holiday and half term activities.

LEISURE ACTIVITIES

There is a wide range of activities available throughout the city and surrounding areas, some of which are offered as short courses. It would be impractical to try to list everything, but there are databases which hold up to date information at Plymouth City Library (see page 77) and the Plymouth Children's Information Service (see page 85) Also check out your neighbourhood project (page 87), sport and leisure centres (page 74). See also Resource Centres (page 77) for further information relating to activities for schools, groups, etc.

BOOKS AND STORYTELLING

Bookstart is a national scheme, which encourages parents to share books with their children from an early age, by offering free books to every child and relevant advice to every parent. The scheme works by presenting parents/carers with a Bookstart pack that includes free books, a nursery rhyme placemat, advice on sharing books, information about library facilities and activities and an invitation to join. Parents usually receive the pack from their Health Visitor at the baby's 7 - 9 month developmental check. For more information, please contact Sue Mills, Bookstart Co-ordinator, Tel (01752) 306791

Plymouth Children's Book Group: One of a number of such groups around the country, which is part of the Federation of Children's Book Groups. For anyone interested in finding out more about good children's books, whether parents, teachers or other professionals. Activities appeal to adults/families. Offers a varied range of events, e.g. meetings to discuss books, author visits, story-time, family activities, etc. Contact Alison Clibbens (01752) 511716 or Michelle Taberner (01752) 262338

Anne Adeney - Author Visits: Tel: (01752) 218344/216788. Anne is well-known in the Plymouth area as an award-winning wooden toymaker. She has now changed direction and is a journalist and writer, mainly of children's books. She is available to give talks and workshops in libraries, clubs and schools. For more information visit her website at www.anne-adeney-author.co.uk

The Storybox Storyteller: Tel: (01752) 569244. A very experienced storyteller and storymaker, specialising in stories for young children and across the primary age range.

Feedback - Free book review magazine: Magazine compiled by city students aged 14 to 18 and distributed free to every school in Plymouth. (see also Children's Library Service page 77)

CHURCHES

The policy of churches towards welcoming children into their services varies as some like them to be part of the congregation from birth whereas others offer separate facilities for children during part or all of the service. Many churches run playgroups, parent and toddler groups, youth clubs, choirs and other activities. There is not room to list all churches in Plymouth; the major denominations list their churches in the telephone directory. For further details about local churches and associated societies on the Internet, go to www.parents-guide-to-plymouth.co.uk/activity.htm

DANCING

There are many dancing schools offering ballet, tap, disco and ballroom dancing. Some require payment termly and others at each session. There is not room to include them all here; they can be found in Yellow Pages. Also, many of the community centres around the city offer a variety of dance classes for children.

MUSIC

Most traditional music teachers like to wait until a child is 5 or 6 years old or can read, although some may be willing to teach a younger child who is musically gifted. Names of local music teachers can be obtained from Yellow Pages and the Plymouth Central Library Music Department.

Laira Youth Band: Contact Mr Tony Hollick Tel: (01752) 216784. Young musicians welcomed from 8 to 18 years - any standard. Performances at charity concerts, fetes, competitions, carnivals, church services, etc.

Musical Playtime: Music and movement classes with a difference for babies and toddlers 8 months – under 4 years. Sessions run during school terms in the following areas: Woolwell, Peverell, Elburton. Contact Julia (01752) 291997 for further information.

Musikgarten: Ivybridge. Pre-school music and movement programme which runs in term time. Singing, musical instruments, movement, listening time, imaginary play, drama and dance. Contact Mervyn Bedford Tel: (01363) 82913 for further information.

Plymouth Music Zone: Raglan Road, Devonport, Plymouth, PL1 4NQ. Tel: (01752) 213690 Currently working with over 2000 children across Plymouth, providing out of school hours music activities across Plymouth, organised through schools. The National Foundation for Youth Music is currently funding the Plymouth Training Orchestra (for students in the early stages of learning an instrument), Plymouth Youth Orchestra (for more experienced students) and Plymouth Youth Choir (for year 7 and above) and a Soul Band. All these activities are free and open access. For further information go to www.parents-guide-to-plymouth.co.uk/activity.htm

Plymouth Musical Activities Club: Contact Mrs Johns Tel: (01752) 700510 Music for fun; children from 9 to 18 years; guitar group (will take complete beginners); small percussion and flute groups. Also have a singing group.

The Soundhouse: Estover Community College, Miller Way, Estover, Plymouth Tel: (01752) 207920. A music centre which focuses on young people, but works across a very wide age range, from 8 years upwards. Offers music workshops, ensemble creations, training, etc. For further information go to www.parents-guide-to-plymouth.co.uk/activity.htm

West Devon Music Centre: Meet at The Ridgeway School, Moorland Road, Plympton, Plymouth. Contact: Nigel Birt at Devon Youth Music Tel: (01392) 385600. Plymouth Youth Wind Band; guitar ensemble. Youngsters are welcomed from 7 - 8 years after they have been learning an instrument for at least a few months.

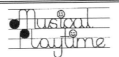

Music and Movement classes with a difference for babies and toddlers from 8 months to under 4 years

Helps communication, co-ordination and confidence through musical fun and enjoyment. Adults also have a good time! Birthday parties too!

For more information contact Julia on (01752) 291997

Maestro's Music Ltd: 52 Ebrington Street, Plymouth. Tel: (01752) 263069. Large variety of musical instruments and accessories; student discount cards available. Also offer music lessons and have a list of qualified music teachers.

(See also Second Hand Goods for details of used musical instrument suppliers page 13)

NATURE

Dartmoor National Park Authority: Ranger Ralph has a club for chidren aged 12 and under, which offers a free membership pack and occasional activities especially for members, together with a quarterly newsletter packed with information, puzzles and competitions. To apply, send four second class stamps with your name, address and age to Ranger Ralph, Dartmoor National Park Authority, Parke, Bovey Tracey, Newton Abbot, TQ13 9JQ. Tel: (01626) 832047 for further information.

The Groundwork Trust: Part of a national environmental initiative sponsored by local and central government and local business and supported by the community. It carries out projects which improve the environment of both urban areas and the surrounding countryside, involving local people. There are opportunities for families to become involved in practical projects; also the Trust works with local schools on specific projects. Contact the Trust at Crownhill Fort Road, Plymouth, PL6 5BX. Tel. (01752) 217721.

Wildlife Watch - Groups at Plymouth, Tavistock, Wembury and Burrator: Contact Devon Wildlife Watch Officer at 35 St David's Hill, Exeter. Tel: (01392) 279244 for details of your local group - the Junior branch of the Devon Wildlife Trust. Members receive a national magazine six times a year and an annual local newsletter. The local groups are involved in environmental activities and some practical conservation work. For children from 7 years to teenage.

Wembury Watch Group: Contact Jo Swift on (01752) 759985. Meets once a month for environmental and educational activities on the third Sunday of the month 2.00 - 4.00 pm at the Wembury Marine Centre. Suitable for 6 - 11 year olds and costs £2 per session or join for a year for £12. (Wembury Marine Centre is closed from October to end March.)

Rockpool Rambles are organised by the Devon Wildlife Trust at Wembury Marine Centre, on Wembury Beach, near Plymouth (map ref: SX518484). For further details of the Centre and events Tel. (01752) 862538.

South Hams Coast and Countryside Service: aims to help visitors and local people to enjoy and gain greater understanding of the South Devon Area of Outstanding Natural Beauty (AONB) and the rest of the South Hams through their events programme and walking and cycling guides to the area. Walks are graded as: 1. Gentle, 2. Moderate, 3. Strenuous. Most events are suitable for family groups - stout shoes or boots should be worn and it is advisable to take a waterproof. For further information Tel: (01803) 861234 ext 1183.

PHAB CLUB

Budoc Phab Club: Meet at Higher St Budeaux Parish Church Hall, Crownhill Road, Plymouth. Contact Ken Clarke Tel: (01752) 263889. Phab Clubs provide leisure and recreational activities for children and young people with a disability, together with able-bodied children and young people, allowing integration in a youth club atmosphere. Juniors are aged 8 to 14 years, and seniors are over 14 years with no upper age limit.

THEATRICAL GROUPS

The groups listed below have an emphasis on youth theatre. There are other theatrical groups in Plymouth which occasionally require children or young people for their productions.

Barbican Theatre: Castle Street, Plymouth, PL1 2NJ.Tel: (01752) 267131. Classes in drama from 5 years up, dance from 3 years up, breakdance from 14 years, ballet from 5 years, static trapeze from 6 years up. The **Plymouth Youth Dance Company** is based at the Barbican Theatre. Also offer dance classes for primary and secondary teachers.

Barbican Theatre Young People's Steering Group: The Barbican Theatre is engaged in a number of projects to involve16 to 25 year olds in theatre and performance arts, including technical and marketing aspects. Kicking Arts is a 10 week chance to find out what the arts are all about. For further information contact Kate Reed Tel: (01752) 242018.

CATS - Children's Amateur Theatre Society: meet on Saturday mornings at St Bartholomew's Church Hall, Milehouse, Plymouth. Acting, singing and some dancing for 3 to approx 16 year-olds, working towards a pantomime or show twice a year; also offer additional lessons in festival and exam work in LAMDA. A second group meets at Kingsbridge. Contact Samantha Groves on (01752) 310263.

Stagecoach Theatre Arts School: Meet at Goschen Centre, Saltash Road, Plymouth. Offer 4 to 16 year-olds three hour sessions where they learn to act, sing and dance. Telephone Frances May on (01752) 701000 for a School Prospectus.

Stage Kids: Sterts Theatre and Environmental Centre, Upton Cross, Liskeard, Cornwall, PL14 5AZ. Tel: (01579) 362382. Youth Theatre

Classes - three groups are run for ages 7 - 18. Phone for further details.

Theatre Royal: Royal Parade, Plymouth, PL1 2TR. Tel: (01752) 230542. The **Young Company**, the UK's largest youth theatre offers young people aged 8 to 25 the opportunity to participate in a wide variety of drama activity. For a small membership fee members are also entitled to large discounts on Theatre Royal shows. The **Tiny Company** is a drama group for 4 to 7 year olds offering fun-filled Saturday mornings. Tel: (01752) 230377. Visit the website at **www.theatreroyal.com**

Totally Crackers Theatrical Department: 15 Beaumont Road, St Judes, Plymouth. Tel: (01752) 663189. Suppliers of props, costumes and make-up for theatrical productions. Visit the website at **http://www.totallycracker.clara.net**

Touchwood Musical Company: Meet regularly and stage musicals, revues and pantomimes. Welcome children aged 7 to 16 years as well as adults. Telephone David Bailey on (01752) 600230

Wranglers Children's Theatre Group: Meet regularly. Telephone D Sullivan on (01752) 302531 or e-mail thewranglers@btinternet.com for details.

UNIFORMED YOUTH ORGANISATIONS

These are international organisations, offering a wide range of indoor and outdoor activities, usually linked to badges, awards, certificates, etc. Many offer local, national and even international camps and there can be the opportunity for community service. Children often like to attend these organisations with their friends. However, if parents are unable to locate a suitable group, the following people will be happy to deal with queries about groups in the area.

Air Training Corps - Plymouth & Cornwall: Officer Commanding, Plymouth & Cornwall Wing ATC, RAF St Mawgan, Newquay, Cornwall. e-mail whq_plymouth@lineone.net. Tel: (01637) 857638. There are 27 locations in Plymouth, West Devon and Cornwall covering: flying, shooting, adventure training, sport, Duke of Edinburgh Award, gliding, visits to RAF stations, summer camps home and abroad. Open to boys and girls between 13 and 18 years of age.

Guides: There are two Divisional Commissioners in Plymouth. For Plymouth East contact Mrs Tessa Ricketts on (01752) 664952; for Plymouth West contact Mrs Brenda Rendle on (01752) 703355. Rainbows: 5 - 7 years, Brownies: 7 - 10 years, Guides: 10 - 14/15 years, Senior Section: 15 years up.

St John Ambulance: 2 Bedford Terrace, North Hill, Plymouth. Tel:

(01752) 665802. Junior youth groups - 6 to 11 years and 10 to 18 years. The groups' activities include first aid, home nursing, home safety, nursing, infant and child care. There are groups at Crownhill, Plymstock, North Hill, St Budeaux, Leigham, Widewell, Lee Moor.

Scouts: Meet at a number of venues around the city. For more information on local groups contact the Scout District office. Tel: (01752) 773717. Beavers: 6 - 8 years, Cubs: 8 -10 years, Scouts: 10 -15 years, Explorer Scouts: 15 years up.

Sea Cadets: TS Golden Hind. Tel: (01752) 555365 and TS Manadon Tel: (01752) 313122 Juniors - 10 to 12 years; Cadets - 12 to 18 years; Marine Cadets - 13.5 to 18 years.

YOUTH ACTIVITIES AND INFORMATION

Duke of Edinburgh Award Scheme: Devon area office - 2 Fore Street, Moretonhampstead Tel: (01647) 440983 The Duke of Edinburgh Award Scheme is open to young people between the ages of 14 and 23 and is run by a number of centres in the city. Phone for details of your nearest centre and for further information about the scheme.

Plymouth Young People's Agenda 21: PYPA 21 is an independent organisation that is supported by Plymouth City Council. Its overall purpose is to help the young people of Plymouth to get involved in 'Agenda 21', the international framework for sustainable development that was agreed to by the world's governments at the 'Earth Summit' in Rio de Janeiro. PYPA 21's task is to initially create awareness amongst the younger generation of Plymouth of 'Agenda 21' and then to gather information from them about what these concerns might be; it is this principle that forms the 'backbone' of PYPA 21. In the summer PYPA21 runs the 'Out and About' series which are relaxed and informal, designed to get young people out enjoying the countryside. Travel is by public transport to show young people what they can do on their own. For further information contact Bran Howell on (01752) 304575

The Princes Trust: COPTE, Picquet Barracks, Cumberland Road, Devonport, Plymouth, PL1 4HX. Tel: (01752) 306146 Drop in to learn more Mon - Fri 9.00 to 4.00. Young people aged 16 - 24 can join a 60 day team course, including motivation, confidence, work and team skills, and community projects. Great fun and outdoor activities including rock climbing, abseiling and caving.

Youth Clubs: There are many youth clubs located around the city. To find a local club contact the one of the Plymouth Area Youth Work Managers at locations around the city (see page 95), check out the Neighbourhood Projects and Community Centres in chapter 4, contact your nearest

Leisure Centre, try the City Library database (see page 76) or check with the churches in your locality.

SPORTS

The City has many sports clubs and facilities. The major and purpose-built centres are listed below, but so many sports clubs exist in the city that it is impractical to list all of them. Parents are recommended to contact Plymouth City Council for specific details of sports in which they are interested, as they keep a contact list of representatives from all sports in the city from angling to yachting, badminton to rugby, boxing to horse-riding, etc. Tel: (01752) 307008. Plymouth City Library also has a database of activities including sports in the city (see page 77).

PLYMCARD

A discount Leisure Card giving holders access to discounted admission, shopping and services at businesses and facilities throughout the City and surrounding area. Any Plymouth City resident aged 5 and over is eligible to apply. In person at First Stop (Civic Centre), or the City Museum Shop or branch libraries. By email to lifelong.learning@plymouth.gov.uk or by post to Plymcard Office, Department for Lifelong Learning, City of Plymouth, PL1 2AA. Check out the website at **www.plymouth.gov.uk/content-1982** Tel: (01752) 307001

PLYMOUTH ADVISORY SPORTS COUNCIL (PASC)

PASC is an umbrella organisation for sports representatives in partnership with Plymouth City Council. Currently there are over thirty sports organisations represented on the general committee. As the local sports council PASC is a sports lottery consultee and its views on lottery grant applications are sought. PASC is a source of information for sports contacts, grant information, Plymouth's sports strategies, sporting events and much more. Contact James Coulton, Head of Community Leisure and Learning, Department for Lifelong Learning, Plymouth City Council, Plymouth, PL1 2AA. Tel: (01752) 307013

Bowling

Megabowl offers ten pin bowling at two centres in Plymouth: Barbican Leisure Park, Coxside Tel: (01752) 252171 and Plymouth Road, Plympton Tel: (01752) 336666.

Canoeing

See Sailing (p 72) and Dartmoor (p 71)

Cricket

Artificial and grass pitches are located throughout the City and are available for seasonal hire by clubs or for use on a casual basis. Details from the DSD Park Services Department. Tel: (01752) 304840/304843.

DISCOUNT CARD

Plymouth Residents <u>Save Money</u> on
Sports • Leisure • Hobbies • Services • Shopping
• Dining Out • Hotels • Health & Beauty

*Plymcard is FREE to children aged 5 – 16, students
and trainees, over 60's and those in receipt of benefit,
or costs only £3 annually
Can be used in 150 local businesses!*

HOW CAN I APPLY FOR A PLYMCARD?

BY PHONE: • Plymcard Infoline (01752) 307001
BY EMAIL: • lifelong.learning@plymouth.gov.uk
BY POST: • Plymcard Office, Lifelong Learning,
Plymouth City Council, Plymouth PL1 2AA

DOWNLOAD AN APPLICATION VIA THE WEB:
• www.plymouth.gov.uk/content-1985

IN PERSON: • Central Lending Library, North Hill
• Plymouth Branch Libraries
• City Museum Shop, North Hill
• First Stop Desk, Civic Centre
• Windsor House, Tavistock Road

Cycling

There are cycle paths at various points through the city and recreational cycle ways (eg in the Plym Valley). For information on cycling in Plymouth or for a copy of the Plymouth Cycle Guide please contact the Transport & Planning Service, Road Safety Team, Plymouth City Council, Civic Centre, Floor 10, Plymouth, PL1 2EW, Tel (01752) 307730 or email roadsafety@plymouth.gov.uk. Copies of the guide are also available from most bike shops, libraries and tourist information centres in Plymouth.

Dartmoor - Outdoor Activities

Plymouth Outdoor Education Centre: Tel: (01752) 406444. Offer adventure activities during the Easter and Summer school holidays and half terms, including adventure days on Dartmoor; kayaking and canoeing days; gorge walking; caving; climbing and abseiling.
See also Nature page 65

Football and Hockey

Pitches are located throughout the city, mainly in large parks and playing fields and are available for either seasonal or casual hire. Contact DSD Park Services Department. Tel: (01752) 304840/304843.
There are all weather floodlit pitches at Manadon and Brickfields, available to hire. Contact the Mayflower Leisure Centre Tel: 0870 3000400
Special Football Development Trust: Set up by parents for players with a disability, for adults and children over 8 years. The Trust is supported by Plymouth City Council Sports Development Unit and Devon County FA. Tel: (01752) 307035.
Plymouth Argyle Football Club: Home Park, Plymouth. Tel: (01752) 562561. Offer Junior Green membership to supporters under 16 years. Also run a scheme "Football in the Community", offering coaching days during the school holidays. For more information telephone the club or visit www.parents-guide-to-plymouth.co.uk/holacts.htm

Gymnastics

Gym Tots For children from crawling to 12 years. Based at Central Park Pool. Tel: Plymouth City Sports on (01752) 607206

There are also many classes for pre-school children at the leisure centres (see page 74).

Horse Riding

Riding Schools:
Most are listed in Yellow Pages. For details of establishments which are inspected and approved by the British Horse Society see www.parents-guide-to-plymouth.co.uk/sports2.htm The BHS Website also offers guidance on what to look for in a riding school.

Plymouth Group Riding for the Disabled Association: Contact Mrs Gilbert Tel: (01752) 707057. Provides riding lessons for children and adults with special needs. Funded by donations.

Ice Skating
Plymouth Pavilions: Millbay Road, Plymouth. Tel: (01752) 222200. Freeform ice rink. Sessions include - family skate; disco skate; monthly session for people with special needs.
Lessons are available for children and adults (from toddler up). Discounts for members of Pavilions PALs. Check out the Website at **www.plymouthpavilions.com**.

Roller Hockey
Plymouth Roller Hockey Club has minor, junior and senior teams from 9 years up, including 3 girls who play for England. Training takes place at the YMCA Kitto Centre in Honicknowle. The club is run by parents. For more details contact Phil on (01752) 844769.

Sailing
Mount Batten Sailing and Watersports Centre: 70 Lawrence Road, Plymouth, PL9 9SJ. Tel: (01752) 404567. Offers a spectacular venue for a large range of sporting and outdoor activities, including residential courses in reasonably-priced accommodation. There are changing rooms, hot showers, training rooms, a licensed bar accessible to families and a range of hot meals and snacks. Details of the relevant groups operating from Mount Batten are given below:
Plymouth Outdoor Education Centre: Tel: (01752) 406444. Offer adventure activities during the Easter and Summer school holidays and half terms, including dinghy sailing courses for 11 years and under; start sailing weeks; seamanship and racing skills; kayaking and canoeing days; coasteering; gorge walking; multi-activity watersports week; windsurfing.
Port of Plymouth Canoeing Association: Canoe and Kayak Club offer introductory courses for adults and children over 12 years. Families are

especially welcome. Apply to
Kayaks and Paddles, Unit 2, The
Western Hangar, Lawrence Road,
Mount Batten, Plymstock,
Plymouth, PL9 9SJ. Tel: (01752)
484004.

Plymouth Sailing School: Queen
Anne's Battery Marina, Plymouth.
Tel: (01752) 667170. Children are
able to undertake land-based
navigation courses and classroom activities. They can only go on to the
water if accompanied by a parent or legal guardian. Also offer family
sailing holidays.
Canoe Adventures: 1 Church Court, Harberton, Totnes, TQ9 7UG. Tel:
(01803) 865301 Offer canoe trips in 12-seater open canoes, along the
rivers of South Devon.

Information on predicted tide times can be found via a link to the UK
Hydrographic Office Tidal Prediction Service at www.parents-guide-to-
plymouth.co.uk/beaches.htm

Skateboarding
There are skateboard parks at Beaumont Park St Judes, Chaddlewood
Park, Plympton and a small one at Central Park. For further information
on parks and their facilities contact DSD Park Services Department on
(01752) 304840/304843.
The City Council is hoping to provide a youth park at Central Park for 12 to
25 year-olds with provision for skate-boarding. Subject to planning and
funding the park is planned for early summer 2004. For further information
Tel: (01752) 307859.

Ski-ing
Plymouth Ski Centre: Alpine Park, Marsh Mills, Plymouth. Tel: (01752)
600220. The largest dry ski slope in the region. Dry ski-ing and
tobogganing from 4 years of age; snowboarding from 10 years of age.
Group or one to one lessons whatever the weather! Also offer children's
activities during the school holidays. Bar and restaurant.
Plym Ski Kids: Tel: (01752) 364058 A lottery-funded activity, for
disadvantaged children aged 4 to 16 years, taking them to the Plymouth
Ski Centre once a week.

Tennis
All-weather and grass tennis courts are located throughout the city, and
are available for either a block booking or casual use. There is a reduced

rate for children under 16 years of age. For further details contact the DSD Park Services Department. Tel: (01752) 304840/ 304843. There are indoor tennis courts at the Devonshire Health and Racquet Club, Crownhill, Plymouth. Tel: 01752 237000 and at the South Devon Tennis Centre in Ivybridge. Tel: 01752 893700.

Trampolining
For children aged 6 to 15 years, based at Central Park Pool. Tel: (01752) 607206

MULTI-PURPOSE SPORTS CENTRES
There are many and varied sport and social activities carried on at the following Plymouth centres. Telephone for details.
Coombe Dean Sports Hall, Coombe Dean School, Charnhill Way, Elburton, PL9 8ES. Tel: (01752) 403113
Eggbuckland Community College Sports Centre, Westcott Close, Eggbuckland, PL6 5YB. Tel: (01752) 779061
Estover Community College Sports Hall, Miller Way, Estover, PL6 8ON. Tel: (01752) 207894
Fursdon Leisure Centre, Fursdon Barn, Penrith Gardens, Estover. Tel: (01752) 771771
Heles School, Seymour Road, Plympton, PL7 4LT. Tel: (01752) 337193
Lipson Community College, Bernice Terrace, Lipson. Tel: (01752) 263284
Marjon Leisure Centre, Derriford Road, PL6 8BH. Tel: (01752) 636876. Swimming; tennis, squash and badminton courts for hire.
Mayflower Leisure Centre, Central Park, PL2 3DG. Tel: 0870 300 0040
Plymouth Playzone, Christian Mill Business Centre, Crownhill. Tel: (01752) 210210. Family entertainment centre on three floors. Play area, café, bar, party rooms for hire. Ball pools, slides and other play equipment, disco.
Plymstock School Sports Centre, Church Road, PL9 9AZ. Tel: (01752) 402679
Ridgeway Community Sports Centre, Ridgeway School, Moorland Road, PL7 3BH. Tel: (01752) 338373
Sir John Hunt Sports Centre, Lancaster Gardens, Whitleigh, PL5 4AA. Tel: (01752) 201202
Stoke Damerel Community College Sports Centre, Somerset Place, PL3 4BD. Tel: (01752) 556065
Tamarside Sports Complex, Tamarside Community College, Trevithick Road, St Budeaux, PL5 2AF. Tel: (01752) 213951.
YMCA Triangles, Cobourg Street. Tel: (01752) 604455

YMCA Kitto Centre, Honicknowle Lane, PL5 3NG. Tel: (01752) 201918. Many sports activities, including swimming at nearby John Kitto Community College.

INDOOR SWIMMING POOLS

Under five year olds are admitted free at all Plymouth city council pools. Children under eight years of age must be accompanied by an adult. Check opening times and admission prices with individual pools. Further information at **www.plymouth.gov.uk/content-1620**.

Central Park Leisure Pools: Outland Road, Milehouse, Plymouth, PL2 3DG. Tel: 0870 300 0010. Main pool, large teaching pool and diving pool with 1m and 3m spring boards and 5m and 7.5m firm boards. Parent and toddler swimming sessions; swimming lessons from 3 years; children's fun sessions on Saturdays; aqua-natal class; aqua-fit. Professional diving school with lessons for all ages. New feature - Haystack Dryer - for £1 up to 2 adults and 3 children can dry off in 3 or 4 minutes in a hot air "people dryer" on poolside.

Marjon Sport and Leisure: Derriford Road, Derriford, Plymouth. Tel: (01752) 636876. Swimming lessons; parent and toddler sessions; aqua-aerobics; life-saving courses; children's summer sport (in the school holidays). Refreshments. (Part of the College of St Mark and St John)

Meadowlands Leisure Pool: The Wharf, Tavistock, PL9 8SP. Tel: (01822) 617774. A fun pool with water slide and a range of aquatic activities; learner pool. Parent and toddler sessions; swimming lessons; national pool lifeguard course. Refreshments.

Plymouth Pavilions: Millbay Road, Plymouth. Tel: (01752) 222200. Fun pool with flumes, wave machine, children's paddling area, waterfalls, Jacuzzi, children's pools and a wrecked galleon. Parent and toddler sessions; swimming lessons. Family-friendly changing facilities. Check out the website at **www.plymouthpavilions.com**

Plympton Pool: Harewood Park, Plympton, Plymouth, PL7 3AS. Tel: 0870 300 0020. Main and learner pools. Swimming lessons; mother and baby sessions; aqua-natal classes for mums-to-be with qualified midwives; aqua-fit; life-saving courses (including rookie course for juniors); ladies and children's octopush on Saturdays. Vending machine refreshments.

Saltash Leisure Centre: Callington Road, Saltash. Tel: (01752) 840940.

Main and learner pools. Swimming lessons; parent and toddler sessions; children's fun sessions on Saturdays; aquacise (incorporating ante- and post-natal); rookie lifeguard course. Creche facility. Cafe.

Seaton Pool: Brest Road, Crownhill, Plymouth, PL6 5XN. Tel: 0870 300 0030. Swimming lessons (age 3 years to adult). Lifesaving classes. Ladies aquafit. Saturday fun factory for children. Patio area available in

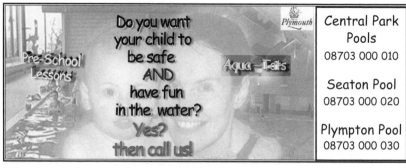

Pre-School Lessons

Do you want your child to be safe AND have fun in the water? Yes? then call us!

Aqua-Tots

Plymouth

Central Park Pools
08703 000 010

Seaton Pool
08703 000 020

Plympton Pool
08703 000 030

the summer for sunbathing/playing. Vending machine refreshments.
South Dartmoor Leisure Centre: St. Leonards Road, Ivybridge. Tel:
(01752) 896999. Swimming lessons; parent and baby sessions and under
five's classes. Also offer Saturday family fun "wet and wild" sessions.
YMCA Kitto Centre: Honicknowle Lane, Plymouth, PL5 3NG. Tel: (01752)
201918. Swimming sessions at nearby John Kitto Community College.

OUTDOOR SWIMMING POOLS
Tinside Lido, Plymouth Hoe PL1 2PA Tel: 0870 300 0042. The Lido opens
for the 2004 season on 29th May through to the beginning of September.
Plymouth City Council offer discounted entry fees to all Plymouth residents
with a Plymcard (see page 69).
Mount Wise Swimming Pool, James Street, Devonport, Plymouth, PL1
4HG. Tel: 0870 300 0042. 2004 Season: 29th May – end of September.
Entry is FREE. Lockers - £1 refundable
There is also a small tidal pool at **Devil's Point**, at the end of Durnford
Street, Stonehouse.

SWIMMING AND DIVING CLUBS
Devonport Royal Swimming Association and Humane Society:
Mr Gregory Tel: (01752) 880153. Swimming teaching from 4 years.
Social swimming, competitions, life-saving, water polo. Meet at Central
Park, Seaton Pool.
Plymouth Diving: Tel: (01752) 607206. Highboard diving for recreation
and competition, for swimmers of all ages from 5 years. Involved in
national and international competition.
Plymouth Leander Swimming Association: Alison Johns Tel: (01752)
516312. Swimming teaching from age 7 years. Competition swimming.
Two coaches with the British swimming coaching team. Meet at Plymouth
College swimming pool.
Plymouth Pisces Swimming Club: Mrs Mary Cole Tel: (01752) 558168.
Open to people of all ages with disabilities and their families. Meet weekly
at Central Park pool for leisure swimming/swimming lessons. Also enter
inter-club galas. Welcome swimming or non-swimming volunteers to
assist.

Port of Plymouth Swimming Association and Humane Society:
Mr Pring Tel: (01752) 771159. Swimming teaching from 4 years; water
polo from 10 years; swimming coaching. Train at the College of St Mark
and St John.

The Evening Herald publishes local swimming reports compiled by their
swimming correspondent, Jon Rudd

LIBRARIES AND RESOURCE CENTRES
Each person using a lending library, whether adult or child, is entitled to a
maximum of 8 books. Adults may borrow books from both the Adults' and
Children's Libraries, but children may borrow only from the Children's
Library (with the exception of older children who may need to borrow adult
books to help with their homework). There is no minimum age for a child's
ticket. All the branch libraries include a children's section. Most of the
libraries offer Storytimes, Rhymetimes and Activities for children. Enquire
at your local library for details of these activities. Turning the Pages, a fun
reading programme in three parts, starting at 5 years, operates from all the
City libraries.

Pre School settings and Childminders may apply for a block loan ticket
enabling them to borrow a small collection of books for up to 6 weeks.
They may also visit the library for special storytime sessions and to
exchange books. Schools are encouraged to hold class visits to the
library incorporating storytimes, exchange of books and introductory
lessons in how the library works and how to find a book.

As well as various different types of books (board books, picture books,
novels, stories for younger readers, non-fiction) the larger libraries also
hold story tapes for children.

Branch Libraries: The telephone number of your local branch library and
specialist library services such as Local History, Music and Drama and
Reference are in the telephone directory listed under Plymouth City
Council, Community Leisure and Learning. Go to www.parents-guide-to-
plymouth.co.uk/resource.htm for direct links to the PCC Library website.

Barbican Theatre: Castle Street, Barbican. Tel: (01752) 267131. The
Barbican Theatre is a nationally acclaimed Theatre-in-Education and
Drama Teaching Service, funded by Plymouth City Council, The Arts
Council of England and South West Arts. The Barbican Theatre travels
around schools in the area seeking to develop the use of drama and
theatre skills for learning, therapy and recreation. They can offer their
services to most groups including pre-school playgroups and special
needs children. At their Barbican Theatre base they offer many facilities
including a number of Youth Theatre opportunities, under professional

guidance, for children of a wide age range; a venue for professional touring productions of special interest to young people; dance and choreography for 3 years old up; arts training programmes for 16 - 25 year-olds and much more! Phone for further details.

Christian Resources Project: 14 Lipson Road, Plymouth. Tel: (01752) 224012. A registered charity promoting Christian education. Open to all schools and churches. Mon to Fri 9 am - 5 pm; Sat 10 am - 4 pm.

The Legendary Weaver

Book & CD package by

Abimbola Alao

Travel back in time to meet Kike, a young heroine who battled disability to become an African legend as the originator of Cornrow, an ancient African hair braiding design. A great book to introduce children & adults to the rich West African culture, together with a CD of African songs.

Available from WH Smith, In Other Words, Waterstones, Amazon.co.uk or by mail order at www.lampoeducation.co.uk

Dartmoor National Park Education Service: Parke, Haytor Road, Bovey Tracey, Newton Abbot, TQ13 9JQ. Tel: (01626) 832093. The service aims to help and advise students with their studies, pupils with their projects and teachers, lecturers and group leaders to organise visits. It can provide a range of educational materials relevant to Dartmoor. With one month's notice, it is possible to organise guided walks as well as site visits, talks and slide shows. There is more information about the work of the Authority at **www.dartmoor-npa.gov.uk**

Jacolly Puppet Theatre: Kirkella Road, Yelverton, PL20 6BB. Tel: (01822) 852346. Email: theatre@jacolly-puppets.co.uk. A professional touring company which performs for schools, theatres, festivals etc. (No outdoor shows or private parties.) Productions vary in size, style and intended age of audience: Dogworthy series for ages 4-8, includes Devon Road Safety Unit commissioned road safety show, a Christmas special and a National Curriculum based teaching show about the seaside. Astra and the Waste Monster for ages 8-11 was commissioned by Devon County Council and teaches energy saving and caring for the Environment. The Real Bugs Show is funded by the BBSRC and is a co-production with the University of Plymouth. It teaches about mini-beasts and is for ages 7-11. Puppetry workshops for adults and children over 4 years.

Lampo Educational Services: PO Box 185, Woolwell, Plymouth, PL6 7ZN Tel: 07909665951. Abi Alao offers storytelling presentations in schools, colleges and the community as a whole; storymaking workshops for teachers, trainers, parents, clergy etc.; seminars for parents, specialising in storytelling for early years children, and ethno storytelling; also workshops in the creative art of African hair braiding and Afro-

Caribbean cookery. See advert on page 78 for details of a book and CD resource pack by Abi.

Plymouth Play Association, Union Street, Plymouth, PL1 3HE, has the biggest selection of re-usable quality scrap for schools, pre-schools, nurseries, art groups, craft clubs or those who just want to have some fun in Plymouth. With regular deliveries of ripstop, neoprene, card, paper, material, boxes, clear CDs, records, it's great for those interested in arts and crafts. They also run a citywide toy library which offers a variety of toys and equipment available to hire at low prices. If you want to find out more about The Scrapstore project or the resources that are available for hire from The PPA then ring on (01752) 256633. Membership is very reasonably-priced.

Regional Interactive Safety Centre: Plymouth Station, Plymouth, PL4 6AB. Tel: (01752) 601999. The objective of RISC is to create an innovative safety, personal safety, health improvement, crime prevention, and crime reduction Education Action Centre. This initiative brings together community and voluntary sector organisations, statutory agencies and local businesses in collaborative activities which will provide practical methods of tackling the issues raised in Government White Papers supporting the local Health Improvement and Crime Reduction Strategies. RISC is an innovative educational resource centre. They are keen to recruit volunteers to help. For further information visit the website at **www.riscsw.com**

Road Safety Team: Plymouth City Council through the Transport and Planning Services' Road Safety Team is committed to the reduction of casualties on our road network and to continue its programme of measures to improve the safety of all road users through education, training and publicity. Emphasis is placed on reducing child casualties through a number of measures including Safer Journeys to School, Child Pedestrian Training and Cycle Training. The following is a list of some of the activities and resources available from the Road Safety Team.

Pre School Groups:
• Visit from a Road Safety Assistant
• Displays, posters and leaflets
• Child car seat information and advice (Fitsafe/Sitsafe)

Primary Schools:
• Pedestrian Training
• Cycle Training
• Life Skills
• Videos, posters and leaflets

- Highway Code for Young Road Users
- Walk to School Week
- Moving On (transition from primary to secondary)
- Educational resources
- School Travel Plans
- Walking Bus
- Theatre in Education programme

Senior Schools:
- Visual Aids
- Videos, posters and leaflets
- Advanced Cycle Training
- Educational resources
- Walk to School Week
- Pre-Driver training Programme

Enquiries should be directed to the Road Safety Team, Transport & Planning Service, Plymouth City Council, Floor 10, Civic Centre, Plymouth, PL1 2EW Tel:(01752) 307730 or email roadsafety@plymouth.gov.uk

Science and Technology Exploratory Garden, Seymour House, Mount Wise, Devonport, Plymouth. Tel: (01752) 605608. Seymour House offers local children the opportunity to enjoy the magnificent 360 degree view of Plymouth Sound and the Royal William Yard with the first camera obscura south-west of Bristol (seen at its best on a sunny day!). The beautiful gardens with sea views house an environmentally-friendly classroom which is an energy-efficient, timber-framed building with a turf roof. It is powered by a wind turbine and solar panels. The idea is to create a hands-on outdoor learning centre of excellence to inspire and motivate youngsters. Available to be booked by school groups and other groups of children and young people. Seymour House is managed by Tamar Education Business Partnership, which promotes and supports a range of mutually-beneficial activities between education, the community and employers.

Stiltskin: is a performance and visual arts company, offering workshops within your community, as well as street performance, site-specific and arts based work. They combine circus, fooling and physical theatre to inspire the imagination, with vibrant, spectacular characters who have a story to tell. They offer a wide range of creative and fun workshops within the visual and performing arts for both children and adults, including circus skills, drama, mask making, carnival puppets and lanterns, mural painting, mosaic making, environmental arts and much more. For further information contact Iain or Jacqueline on (01752) 366062.

TOY LIBRARIES

A number of the neighbourhood centres listed in Chapter 4 run toy libraries for local families. (See page 87)

North Plymouth Family Centre Toy Library, 3 Crownhill Road, Plymouth, PL6 5AG. For ages 0 – 5 years Tel: (01752) 787800

Plymouth Play Association, Union Street, Plymouth, PL1 3HE, run a citywide toy library which offers a variety of toys and equipment available to hire at low prices. Tel: (01752) 256633.

FAMILY SUPPORT ORGANISATIONS INCLUDING HEALTH AND WELFARE SERVICES

ADVICE AND INFORMATION SERVICES

There are many databases set up by organisations in Plymouth and this section aims to point you in the direction of someone who can help with specific issues. Many weblinks to other databases on the Internet are available at www.parents-guide-to-plymouth.co.uk/advice.htm. The principal source of information on advice and support services in Plymouth is the Plymouth Local Information System for Parents. (see page 85) (See also Family Support p 97)

Child Support Agency: Crownhill Court, Tailyour Road, Crownhill, Plymouth, PL6 5UE. Tel: (01752) 761600. Deals with child support applications, collecting, processing applications and imposing assessments. Offers advice and interview service for customers and help with completion of CSA forms.

Citizen's Advice: Virginia House, 40 Looe Street, The Barbican, Plymouth. Tel: (01752) 207088. Open on Monday 10.00 am - 3.00 pm, Tuesday 10.00 am - 1.00 pm, Thursday 10.00 am - 3.00 pm. A free, independent and non-judgemental source of information and advice on a wide range of subjects including housing, consumer, tax and personal problems, benefits, health and social services, legal aid and local facilities. Citizens Advice offers community legal services. It aims to promote equal opportunities and anti-discrimination.

Connexions Cornwall and Devon is the partnership that is delivering the information, advice, guidance and personal support service for all 13 – 19 year olds (24 years if with additional or special needs), known as the Connexions Service. Its aim is to make a real difference to young people encouraging them to continue and succeed in learning whether in full-time education or training while at work. All 13 – 19 year olds have access to Connexions through a Personal Adviser. This may be in school, in further or higher education or in or out of work. The Personal Adviser is their single point of contact who can bring together those organisations who work with young people to provide co-ordinated and improved help and support. Staff in Connexions centres give clear information and advice about careers, educational courses, training and employment. They can also direct young people to additional help on health, benefits, housing and any other issue that may prevent them from continuing in learning. For more information ring freephone 0800 97 55 111 to make an appointment to see a Connexions Personal Adviser.

Devon Law Centre: Virginia House, 40 Looe Street, Plymouth, PL4 0EB. Tel: (01752) 519794. Offer legal advice and representation in housing, education, community care, and immigration law.

Disability Information and Advice Centre (DIAC): Ernest English House, Buckwell Street, Bretonside, Plymouth. Tel: (01752) 201065 Local Information and advice on all aspects of disability; database of local support groups.

Frank: For information and advice about drugs and alcohol, call FREEPHONE 0800 776600 or go to www.talktofrank.com. (see also Family Support page 97)

Naval Personal and Family Service: Fenner Block, HMS Drake, Plymouth, PL2 2BG. Tel: (01752) 555041 Provides professional social work, community work and support services for Royal Naval personnel and their families/dependents. Referral by self, family or other agencies.

NSPCC:
Child Protection Helpline: Tel: 0808 800 5000. A free 24 hour service, available 24 hours a day, 365 days a year, which provides counselling, information and advice to anyone concerned about a child at risk of abuse. A qualified social work counsellor will listen to a caller's concerns and decide with the caller if action is required. If appropriate, the NSPCC will contact social services or the police. The NSPCC continually seeks to maintain high standards. Some calls may be recorded to ensure that the counsellors give the best possible service. A call will not be recorded without permission.
Devon and Cornwall Young Witness Support Project. Supports young people giving evidence in criminal trials in Devon, Plymouth and Cornwall. Devon Child Protection Centre. The centre works with adults who pose a

NAVAL PERSONAL FAMILY SERVICE (NPFS)

NPFS is based in HMS DRAKE, the Naval Base in Plymouth, providing a wide range of services including:

A comprehensive and professional Social Work service to service personnel and their families. Referrals can be from the serving personnel, their families or other agencies.

Community Services

A number of Community Centres and Community Houses are available on the largest of the Service Family Accommodation (formerly Married Quarters) estates.

Centres are sited at Crownhill, Plympton, Plymstock and Torpoint. A Community house is sited at Widewell.

These offer a wide range of activities including **Parent & Toddler** Groups, **Adult Education**, various **Keep Fit** groups, **Youth Clubs**, **Social activities** and **Holiday Playschemes** for the children. See the article Royal Naval Community Centres for telephone numbers.

Sailors & Families Advice Bureau (SAFAB) - The

Navy's equivalent to a CAB - Jacqui or Lynn will be happy to respond to any question (01752) 569696.

Alexandra House

Alexandra House, sited at Crownhill is an independent registered Charity providing residential or day care for service children. They work very closely with NPFS and other Service Welfare providers. More information available from NPFS (01752) 555041.

risk of sexual harm to children and young people, in order to prevent abuse. The centre also works with children and young people who display sexually harmful behaviour.

Plymouth Children's Information Service: The Children's Information Service provides a unique service for parents, providers of childcare and all those involved with Early Years care. Their aim is to ensure that you have access to accurate and up-to-date information. They offer free, impartial guidance and information on a full range of children's services, resources and issues, led by the needs of children and their families, carers, employers, professionals, the local and national Government and their agencies. They have a database of childcare providers including day nurseries, pre-schools, child minders, holiday schemes, out of school care and more. They can also give guidance for lone parents, benefits information, working tax credit, training and recruitment, returning to work and what to look for when choosing a childcare provider. For providers of childcare they can offer advice on childcare business planning, childcare training, the registration process, setting-up of new provision and sign posting to other agencies. If you think that the Children's Information Service can help you, they welcome your call on FREEPHONE 0800 783 4259.

Plymouth City Council Access Consultants: Department for Regeneration, Civic Centre, Royal Parade, Plymouth. Tel: (01752) 304577 Provides a source of information on all aspects relating to access for those with mobility problems, sensory impairment or other similar difficulties, including Transport, Shopping, Public Conveniences, Car Parking, Visitor Attractions, General Contacts.

Plymouth City Central Library, Drake Circus, Plymouth. Tel: (01752) 305907 Keeps a database of local clubs and societies, music teachers and groups and provides a general information service. Accessible via branch libraries throughout the city or via the website at www.parents-guide-to-plymouth.co.uk/resource.htm

Plymouth and District Racial Equality Council: 40 Looe Street, Plymouth, PL4 0EB. Tel: (01752) 312640 Advice and support for members of Plymouth's ethnic minority communities. The N'Deagainsia Project is jointly managed by NCH Action for Children and the Racial Equality Council who work together to deliver support services for black children and young people, their families and carers. The annual Respect Festival aims to bring together ethnic minority groups in celebration and help counteract racism in the city.

Plymouth Guild of Voluntary Service: Ernest English House, Buckwell Street, Plymouth, PL1 2DA. Tel: (01752) 201766 Incorporating the Volunteer Centre, Women's Refuge, Hearing and Sight Centre and the

Disability Information and Advice Centre (see page 83)

Plymouth Local Information Service for Parenting: A comprehensive directory held by the Plymouth Parent Partnership Service (see page 61) which lists services offering information, education and support for parenting. Currently accessible via the Parents Guide to Plymouth website at www.parents-guide-to-plymouth.co.uk/plisp.htm

Plymouth Primary Behaviour Support Team: Tel: (01752) 770050 Part of the Department for Lifelong Learning, offering a range of services to parents across Plymouth. The multi-agency team is led by a Senior Educational Psychologist and includes support workers, social workers, teachers and secretarial support. The team is experienced in working with individual primary school children, class groups, schools and families. See also Plymouth Psychology Service on page 59

Parent Teacher Association for Plymouth, Torbay and Devon: Tel: Laura Foley on (01752) 671363 Offer information, advice and support to parents and schools through newsletters, telephone advice, personal contact, seminars, conferences on issues ranging from improving home/school links, parenting education, bullying in schools, charity registration, etc.

Plymouth Tourist Information - Discovery Centre: Crabtree (Marsh Mills Roundabout), Plymouth, PL3 6RN. Tel: (01752) 266030/266031 Plymouth Tourist Information Centre: Island House, 9 The Barbican, Plymouth, PL1 2LS. Tel: (01752) 304849. See also page 36.

Samaritans: 20 Oxford Place, Plymouth, PL1 5AJ. Tel: 08457 909090; e-mail jo@samaritans.org 24-hour telephone service for people experiencing feelings of emotional distress, including those of suicide. People may also meet the Samaritans and talk in confidence at their offices between 10 am and 10 pm. Although originating in the Anglican church it is not a religious organisation. If appropriate and with the caller's permission they will refer callers to other organisations who may be able to help with a specific problem.

Youth Enquiry Service: 14-16 Union Street, Derrys Cross, Plymouth, PL1 2SR Tel: (01752) 206626. Offers a wide range of free, confidential services for 13 to 25 year olds, including counselling, general support, sexual health, personal development, help with accommodation, etc.

NEIGHBOURHOOD PROJECTS

The following centres offer a wide range of services and activities for families within their local community, and are keen to work with local people to satisfy the needs of the area. The items listed for each centre give a general description of what is offered at the time of publication, but there may well be other activities that are not listed. The services may only be available on certain days, so it is best to phone for further information before going to the Centre. There are many other community centres around the city, offering adult education classes, sports activities, youth clubs, etc.

Devonport Parent and Children's Project
Leander House, Fore Street, Devonport, PL1 4DW Tel: (01752) 565555. Offers:
* Short courses (free) on topics around family issues
* Groups offering help, advice, information, play opportunities, support, etc for parents/carers and young children.
* Men's group for all dads and male carers, offering friendship, support, toy loan, group discussions.
* Toy library

Devonport Regeneration Company
38 – 40 Marlborough Street, Devonport, Plymouth, PL1 4AP. Tel: (01752) 562518. Offers an information and advice service, including help with benefit problems; also run family support projects. The aim is to provide better social, health, leisure and educational facilities in the Devonport area.

East End Partnership
Plymouth City Council have declared the area encompassing Cattedown, Prince Rock and Coxside as the East End Renewal Area. This is intended to bring about comprehensive regeneration in this area, with plans to

provide a new community centre and better health, social, leisure and educational facilities throughout the area.

Residents receive regular newsletters keeping them up to date with developments. If you require further information contact the East End Renewal Area Office, 4 Mainstone Avenue, Cattedown; PL4 9NB. Tel: (01752) 306525 or email eera@plymouth.gov.uk.

Efford Youth and Community Centre
Blandford Road, Efford, PL3 6HU Tel: (01752) 776853. Offers:
- Parent and toddler group
- Junior youth clubs
- Family workshops
- ICT and basic skills for parents and their children
- Information, advice, help
- Adult education

Frederick Street Centre
Frederick Street West, Stonehouse, PL1 5JW. Tel: (01752) 228906. Offers:
- Parent and toddler group
- Youth activities
- Play schemes
- Young mothers drama and support group
- Adult learning

Jan Cutting Healthy Living Centre
Scott Business Park, Beacon Park Road, PL2 2PQ. Tel: (01752) 203670. Offers:
- Family Focus with Health Visitor and Parent Worker
- Information, advice and help
- First aid course
- Potential FM – singing and dancing for under-16s
- Exercise sessions
- Café

Keyham Community Partnership
15 Station Road, Keyham, PL2 1NF. Tel: (01752) 500900 Neighbourhood Resource Centre offers:
- Information, advice and guidance on education, informal and formal training, benefits, housing, childcare, health and disabilities
- Community activities
- Links into employment
- Free Internet access and e-mail facility
- Informal community learning
- Homework club
- Learn Direct courses and UK Online
- Photocopying, faxing and laminating facilities

The Morley Youth and Community Centre
Broadlands Gardens, Plymstock, PL9 8TU. Tel: (01752) 404370. Offers:
- Pre-school group
- Breakfast and after school clubs
- Holiday playschemes
- Junior clubs
- Youth clubs
- Adult education
- Sports groups

Mount Gould Neighbourhood Association
Astor Community Centre, Dartmoor View, Mount Gould, PL4 7QG. Tel: (01752) 250991 email: mgnaastorcc@msn.com. Currently offer youth groups, but they are planning to expand community provision. Contact the centre for further information.

Nomony Family Centre
St Johns Bridge Road, Cattedown, PL4 0JJ. Tel: (01752) 667869. Nomony is an Early Excellence Centre that aims to provide an integrated service for children and their families who live in the Prince Rock, Cattedown and Coxside areas of Plymouth. Offers:
- Good quality early education and day care in a warm and friendly setting
- Parent and toddler group
- Workshops with crèche facilities, allowing parents and carers the opportunity to explore such issues as healthy living or developing their parenting skills.
- Access to adult education and training for those parents/carers seeking skills and qualifications for employment

North Plymouth Family Centre
3 Crownhill Road, Crownhill, PL6 5AG. Tel: (01752) 787800. Services

include:
- Parenting groups
- Family contact centre
- Support groups for families and children
- Community casework
- Young people's support group
- Toy library

Radford Community Centre

Radford Community Centre, Stokeinway Close, Plymstock, PL9 9JL. Tel: (01752) 406680. Offers:
- Creche oriented towards service families, but open to civilians
- Parent and toddler group
- Pre-school group
- Youth group
- Parent and child activities and learning
- Support for parents by parents
- Information, advice, help
- Support during times of hardship/crisis
- Respite care

Rees Youth and Community Centre

Mudge Way, Plympton, PL7 2PS. Tel: (01752) 337267. Offers:
- Parent and toddler groups
- Youth groups (ages 7 to 21 years)
- Adult education classes
- Street youth work

Ringmore Way Family Centre

41 Ringmore Way, West Park, PL5 3EQ. Tel: (01752) 351070. Services include:
- "Wooden tops" group for 3-5 years
- Parent and toddler group
- Young carers group for under 8's
- Advice and information for the local community

Roundabout Day Care Centre

Cattedown Roundabout, Plymouth. Tel: (01752) 263880. **Families First** offers:
- Parenting classes for parents of children of all ages
- Parent and baby group
- Parent and toddler group
- Healthy eating project
- Music time group for pre school children and their parents
- Toy library

- Keep fit activities

Southway Centre
Hendwell Close, Southway, PL6 6TB. Tel: (01752) 775969. Offers:
- Support for young parents
- Advice and information
- Parent and baby and parent and toddler groups
- Adult education
- Children's sports activities
- After school club and school holiday playscheme provided by Southway Play Care at the Southway Centre – tel: 703581 for further information.

Sunflower Family Centre
27 Adelaide Street, Stonehouse, PL1 3JG. Tel: (01752) 256359. The Sunflower Centre offers:
- Support for families during times of hardship/ crisis;
- Parent and child activities and learning, normally for parents of children under 5. During the school holidays these are extended to accommodate children up to 8 years.
- Information and advice
- Parenting skills group (by referral)
- Summer outings, Christmas parties, short holiday breaks for families
- Community based Family Support Workers work with families in their own homes

Tamerton Foliot Community Centre
Cunningham Road, Tamerton Foliot, PL5 4PU. Tel: (01752) 772470. Offers:
- Parent and toddler group
- Youth club
- Leisure activities (for adults and children) including dance classes and martial arts

Whitleigh Youth Centre
Lancaster Gardens, Whitleigh, PL5 4AA Tel: (01752) 771210
- Youth clubs
- Parents projects

SURE START
Sure Start is a Government-funded 10 year programme, launched in December 2002 to bring together Government policy on early education, childcare, health and family support. Sure Start offers all children access to free early education before they start school, more and better childcare

and greater help where there is greater need through childcare tax credit, children's centres and Sure Start local programmes. It supports families from pregnancy right through until children are 14, or 16 if they are disabled or have special needs. The information below was correct at the time of going to print, but the Sure Start projects will respond to local needs and should be contacted for details of current activities and to suggest possible topics for action. (See also Sure Start Plus on page 111)

Four Woods is the name for the SureStart programme in the Budshead and Honicknowle wards of Plymouth, which will offer a host of new facilities for local residents in the area.

Programme Manger Heather Reid says that the programme aims to give local young children under 4 years the best start in life with the help and support of their families and partner agencies and over the next ten years well over 5 million pounds will be invested into Four Woods SureStart.

Services on offer at the moment range from:
* children's activities
* indoor/outdoor play opportunities for under 4's
* extra health services including baby clinics, breast feeding support groups, speech and language and baby massage
* Support for families via an outreach/ home visiting service
* Training/learning opportunities
* Extra support for families in times of crisis.
* Coffee mornings offering an informal parent support network run by parents
* Complimentary therapy service which includes aromatherapy, cranial osteopathy and homeopathy.
* Mobile toy library
* Exercise classes
* Additional support for special needs children and their families
* Pre-nursery group
* Summer play scheme
* Drop-ins for parents

The services are delivered from a range of venues across the area, including Ringmore Way Family centre, Bethany Hall, St Francis of Assisi, Woodfield Primary School and

Do you have a child under four years old? Do you live in the Whitleigh, Ernesettle, West Park or Honicknowle area?

If so:

"Sure Start aims to give local children under four the best start in life with the help of their families and others by delivering a range of free services to those living in the area."

Find out if you can become a Sure Start member and start accessing the services today. Ring: 01752 366795

SureStart

Ernesettle Children's centre. The name was chosen by the local community, the staff of Sure Start and the SureStart Partnership Board, because of the woods to be found in both the wards.
If you would like to know more about SureStart Four Woods please call on **(01752) 366795** or pop in for a coffee.

Sure Start Keystone covers the areas of Ford, Keyham, Stoke, Morice Town and Stonehouse. Keystone runs a number of groups, including:
- Ante-natal classes
- Dads' group
- Baby massage
- Drop-in clinics
- Mobile book and toy library

They are very keen to encourage families in the area to join one of the parents forums. As they say "the more the merrier"!
Sure Start Keystone is at 46 Ryder Road, Keyham, Plymouth, PL2 1JA. Tel: (01752) 208345

LARK Sure Start Project is a Sure Start Programme available to all families in the Ham and North Prospect areas of the city, with children aged 0 – 4 years. The following services are offered to families:
Health Visitor: Provides extra health visiting for families experiencing difficulties with their children or family life. Tel: (01752) 511614
Community Paediatrician: Provides a service for children whose parents have concerns regarding their child's general development and health. Tel: (01752) 314350
Speech and Language Therapists: Work with children in their home and at nursery; provide help to children who have difficulties talking and listening Tel: (01752) 510779
Portage Service: Provides a home visiting service which helps parents work with their children who have special needs, developmental skills. Tel: (01752) 314337
Nursery Nurses: Run a free day care creche for local children; work in community settings and family homes providing children with the opportunity to learn new skills through play. Tel: (01752) 213551
Pre-School Advisory Teacher: Provides advice and support to families with children who have special educational needs. Tel: (01752) 314426
Talking Shops: Produces resources and games designed to encourage good listening and speaking skills; organises art and craft workshops where parents can make their own toys and games to take home. Tel: (01752) 313293
Welfare Benefits Advisor: Help with benefits, money and employment rights issues including form-filling, support and appeals; helps with looking at options to get into employment and training. Tel: (01752) 313293

Women's Development Worker: Provides individual and group support, identifying and working on issues important to local women. Tel: (01752) 510666

Domestic Violence Worker: Free confidential service – with information, practical advice, emotional support and access to safe accommodation for women facing domestic violence. Tel: (01752) 512600

Drug and Alcohol Worker: Information, advice and support on any issues regarding drugs and/or alcohol. Tel: (01752) 512600

Job Broker: Advice and information on training, job searching, application forms, CVs and much more. Tel: (01752) 313293

Lark Sure Start Project, 99 North Prospect Road, Plymouth, PL2 2NA.

Tamar F.O.L.K (For Our Local Kids!) is a Sure Start programme covering all families with 0 – 3 year olds, living in Weston Mill, St Budeaux, Kings Tamerton and Barne Barton. "Hot Gossip" is a bi-monthly newsletter providing details of all current activities, listing useful contacts and giving helpful hints. If you live in this area and haven't received any copies, please contact the office on FREEPHONE 0800 0730754. Many things are up and running, from wrap around nursery care to free books for all two year olds, and much more is planned for the future. They are working with local parents and agencies to ensure that all 0 – 3 year olds get the best start in life . . . whatever that might mean for them individually.

Parents' views are highly valued and help shape the programmes provided. There are currently 3 parents forums, where you can informally share your ideas over coffee with other local parents (both mums and dads). These are also places for having fun together in a relaxed environment. Creches are provided so you can bring your pre-school children along with you. "Come and tell us what is important for you and your child so we can try to do something to help you reach your goals." Sure Start Tamar Folk is at 16 Miers Close, Barne Barton, PL5 1BS. FREEPHONE 0800 0730754

Royal Naval Community Centres

Royal Naval Community Centres offer a wide range of family and social activities, ranging from Adult Education, Parent and Toddler Groups, Keep Fit, Thrift Shops, Youth Clubs, etc

Hillcrest Close, Plympton
Tel: (01752) 343225

Crownhill Fort Road, Crownhill Tel: (01752) 779765
Stokingway Close, Plymstock Tel: (01752) 406680
Trevorder Close, Torpoint Tel: (01752) 812399

Royal Naval Pre-school groups are available to all families at
Eggbuckland, Crownhill, Widewell, Horrabridge, Plymstock, Torpoint. For
further details telephone (01752) 782921.
The Naval Community Officer is based at Crownhill and will be happy to
help with additional information. Tel: (01752) 770860.

YOUTH WORK MANAGERS
Youth workers work with young people aged between 11 and 25 in a range
of different settings, including youth clubs and centres, on summer activity
programmes, on the streets and in parks, in schools and colleges and in
special projects. The aim of youth work is to provide young people with
opportunities for personal and social development that enable them to gain
the skills, knowledge and confidence they need to play an active role in
decisions that affect their lives.

The **Acting Principal Youth Officer** for Plymouth is Christine Smith,
based at The Central Youth Work Team, Top Floor Anglia House, Derry's
Cross, Plymouth, PL1 2SH. Tel:
(01752) 306596

The following people are also based at
Anglia House:
**Young People's Participation
Worker (city-wide)
Youth Work Apprenticeship Scheme
Co-ordinator
Youth Development Worker
(Cattedown, Coxside, Barbican,
Prince Rock)**

The **Youth Work Managers** are based
at various venues around the city and
can be contacted at:
**Youth Development Worker
(Devonport, Keyham, Stoke**), c/o
Welcome Hall, 4 Fore Street,
Devonport, PL1 4AH. Tel: (01752)
560374
Eggbuckland Community College,
Hartley House, Charfield Drive,
Eggbuckland, PL5 6PS. Tel: (01752)

adults

Go4

advice about learning and work

Would you like free and
impartial advice to help you:

• make a change?
• learn something new?
• improve your skills?
• find out about training and
  qualifications
• find out about information on
  childcare?
• start some voluntary work?

To find out more call us on the
Go4 Enquiry Line 0845 8 50 50 70
or visit www.go4lw.co.uk

95

767788

Estover Community College, Miller Way, PL6 8UN. Tel: (01752) 207893

Honicknowle Youth & Community Centre, Honicknowle Green, Honicknowle, PL5 3PX. Tel: (01752) 705297

Efford Youth & Community Centre, Blandford Road, Efford, PL3 6HU Tel: (01752) 776853

Lipson Community College, Bernice Terrace, Lipson, PL4 7PG. Tel: (01752) 662997

Trelawney Youth & Community Centre, Ham Drive, PL2 2NJ. Tel: (01752) 362263

Southway Youth & Community Centre, Hendwell Close, Southway, PL6 6TB. Tel: (01752) 775969

Whitleigh Youth Centre, Lancaster Gardens, Whitleigh, PL5 4AA. Tel: (01752) 771210

Harbourside Youth Centre, Savage Road, Barne Barton, PL5 1BY. Tel: 07879417947 (mobile)

Morley Youth & Community Centre, Broadland Gardens, Plymstock, PL9 8TE. Tel: (01752) 404370

Rees Youth & Community Centre, Mudge Way, Plympton, PL7 2PS. Tel: (01752) 337267

Frederick Street Centre, Frederick Street, Stonehouse, PL1 5SX. Tel: (01752) 228906

Tothill Community Centre, Knighton Road, St Judes, PL4 7PG. Tel: (01752) 665919

Woodland Fort Community Centre, Crownhill Road, PL5 3SQ. Tel: (01752) 703180

ADULT EDUCATION

There is a tremendous range of part-time day and evening classes at centres around the city. In July a brochure is sent to every household in the city by the Department for Lifelong Learning. Enquire at your local library or community education centre if you require further information or telephone the Community Learning office on (01752) 660713.

All Children First offer guidance and information for potential childcare and play workers in Plymouth. This involves running a FREE half-day information workshop designed to give candidates all the knowledge they need for making the right decisions about their career, training and funding options. For further information, or to book a place on the workshop, telephone FREEPHONE 0800 195 1712.

Innovative Outreach Community Consortium (10CC) is a new project aiming to bring education right into the community. Tel: (01752) 300201 (See also Family Support Services below)

FAMILY BENEFITS AND RIGHTS

For information about Child Tax Credit telephone The Plymouth Children's Information Service on FREEPHONE 0800 783 4259.

For information and advice about Benefits contact your Jobcentre at: 2-4 Buckwell Street, Plymouth, PL1 2DD Tel: (01752) 616000, 4 Hoegate Street, Plymouth, PL1 2AT Tel: (01752) 616100, 97-99 The Ridgeway, Plympton, Plymouth, PL7 3AX Tel: (01752) 615800 or St Levan Road, Plymouth, PL2 3BD. or any Jobcentre.

Lone Parents requiring advice and who do not have a Lone Parent adviser can contact Karen on (01752) 517485.

FAMILY SUPPORT

Childline: Children requiring counselling. FREEPOST 1111, London N1. Tel: (FREEPHONE) 0800 1111

The Children's Fund – Plymouth Partnership

The Children's Fund provides targeted support for children in the 5-13 age group, and their families to overcome poverty and disadvantage. Examples of the services provided mainly through voluntary and community organisations are: homework clubs, holiday playschemes, counselling, school mediation and sports activities.

For more information contact: Mark Hemmings, Programme Manager Tel: (01752) 300233

CITY OF PLYMOUTH FAMILY PLACEMENT SERVICE

Midland House, City of Plymouth, Plymouth, PL1 2AA. Tel: (01752) 306800

Foster Carers: Carers are needed to provide homes for children and young people who are unable to live at home. You will receive a fostering allowance, dependent upon the child's age, for the cost of caring. There is a need for a range of carers and adopters who reflect the wide range of ethnicities and cultures within our community.

Adopters: The Family Placement Service is looking for people from all walks of life and from different ethnicities and cultures. If you are interested, phone for further information.

Credit Unions

There are four Credit Unions in Plymouth. They operate as a non profit-making community bank for adults and children within their area, for a one-off membership fee of £1. Members save regularly and after 13 weeks adult savers are eligible for a low-cost loan if required. Telephone to check if you are in the qualifying area.

Fortress Credit Union, below Crownhill Baptist Church, 1 Berwick

Avenue, Crownhill, Plymouth, PL5 3TD. Tel: (01752) 201183
Hope Credit Union, Postal address: 51 Quarry Park Road, Peverell, Plymouth, PL3 4LW. Tel: (01752) 668822 e-mail: info@hopecreditunion.co.uk Website: www.hopecreditunion.co.uk
Stonehouse Credit Union 142 Union Street, Plymouth, PL1 3HL. Tel: (01752) 301871
West of Plymouth Credit Union, 14 Cumberland Street, Mount Wise, Plymouth, PL1 4DX. Tel: (01752) 201329

FOSTERING & ADOPTION
01752 306800

FOSTER CARERS are needed to provide homes for children & young people who are unable to live at home. You will receive a fostering allowance, dependent upon the child's age. We are looking for a range of carers and adopters who reflect the wide range of ethnicities and cultures within our community.
INTERESTED IN FOSTERING OR ADOPTION? PLEASE CALL US.

Crossline Helpline:
37 – 41 Grenville Road, St Judes, Plymouth, PL4 9PY Tel: (01752) 666777 Provides a confidential 24 hour helpline for anyone in need. Counselling service by appointment. Service provided by trained Christian listeners and trained counsellors. Also have a support group for parents of young children (0 – 5 years) (PUPS), who for whatever reason, find themselves under pressure.

Families for Children Adoption Agency
Middletons, Wyndham Square, Plymouth, PL1 5EG. Tel: (01752) 256202. Families for Children is the only voluntary adoption agency covering Devon, Cornwall and Dorset, originally set up in 1992 as a joint venture between the Exeter Diocesan Board for Christian Care and the Plymouth Diocesan Catholic Children's Society. In 2003 it became a separate charity in its own right. The main work of Families for Children is to find parents for children who need a new family of their own. The Agency focuses on finding families for children over the age of 5 years and those with disabilities or special placement needs. In some circumstances the Agency may be able to offer support and counselling to pregnant women and their partners who are unsure about the future of their baby. This support may also include practical help such as finding accommodation and helping to sort out financial difficulties. Telephone for further information or to request an information pack.

Family and Parent Learning Services
The Family and Parent Learning Service offers informal learning opportunities to groups of families in schools and community venues in targeted communities across the city. A range of sessions and short

programmes are on offer which include a focus on: children's development and education, family first aid, confidence building, healthy eating, creative art and preparing for the future. The provision is free and particularly suitable for parents wishing to build on their skills and work towards a nationally recognised qualification. Childcare is provided alongside the learning programmes. For more information contact Family and Parent Learning Service on (01752) 256978.

Foster Care Associates

Foster Care Associates (FCA) is a UK wide independent fostering agency whose South West regional office is in Plymouth. The agency recruits, trains and approves foster carers and offers high quality family placements, at a local level, to children and young people who are 'looked after' by local authorities and Social Services Trusts. FCA focuses on providing a service to children and young people who are sometimes described by referring local authorities as 'difficult to place'. This is not a description the FCA particularly welcomes or seeks to define but it is useful in emphasising that the agency receives referrals for placement of children and young people who have complex and complicated histories, make considerable demands of foster carers and whose placements will require intensive support.

FCA is currently seeking to recruit new carers in the Plymouth area. If you would like further information, telephone (01752) 254554.

Harbour Drug and Alcohol Services

For advice and information if you suspect, or know, that your child is using drugs or has a problem with alcohol, contact Harbour Young People's Team Tel: (01752) 206626 or The Harbour Drug and Alcohol Services Tel: (01752) 267431 You can also call FREEPHONE 0800 776600 24 hours a day for information and advice.

Parent to Parent

A training project for parents who wish to have an active role in their community, helping other parents who need befriending. The project is funded by Neighbourhood Renewal Fund, Education Action Zone and Sure Start and runs in areas of the city that benefit from such funding. The aim of the project is to support parents, and enhance the development of children, by working with families and providing guidance through a befriending service. If you are interested in becoming a befriender telephone Fran Owen on (01752) 366400.

Parents Again

C/o Devonport Social Services 'Wolseley', Wolseley Road, Plymouth, PL2 3BW. Tel: (01752) 308980 – David Pitcher, (Social Services) or (01752)

257658. An organisation for helping grandparents who care for their grandchildren as parents. The aims of Parents Again are to:
- Give and receive support by sharing with others in a similar position
- Obtain advice and information that is helpful in bringing up a grandchild
- Raise awareness among professionals and policy makers, and the general public, of the needs of grandparents who care

Plymouth City Council Social and Housing services

The Children and Families Division of Social and Housing Services work with many children and families each year. Whilst the emphasis is on protecting children, social services endeavour to support children and families whenever they can. The CHEN (Children with care, health and educational needs) support families where a child has special needs. The department offers information and advice and services include respite care, fostering and adoption, with Family Centres offering formal and informal support to parents and children. The department also assesses those adults who wish to become foster carers or prospective adopters.

The points of contact are:
Plymouth North, Wolseley House, Wolseley Road, Plymouth. Tel: (01752) 305638
Plymouth South, Gill Akaster House, Lockyer Street, Plymouth. Tel: (01752) 305600

Plymouth Family Support Services

Kinterbury House, Kinterbury Street, St Andrews Cross, Plymouth, PL1 2DG. Tel: (01752) 255106 A team of trained, experienced and supported volunteers. Provide support for families under stress and help develop preventative work within the local community. Provide a Reception Service supporting those who attend Case Conferences in Plymouth. Volunteers are involved in:
- Plymouth family phone-line - an information and listening ear service on (01752) 668686 Monday to Thursday 10.00 am - 12.00 noon
- befriending parents and young people
- independent visitor service for young people in care
- adoption support
- anti-bullying workshops in schools
- extensive programme of training days for people who work with children and families
- undertaking research and developing new initiatives to meet community needs
- counselling - including anger management; lifestory creative therapy
- bereavement support in schools - for children experiencing loss
They are also keen to hear from people willing to volunteer.

Plymouth Mediation: 18 Harwell Street, Plymouth, PL1 5RY. Tel: (01752) 312121. Aims to help parents who are splitting up, to talk through and agree arrangements for the children, rather than argue such decisions out in court.; offers families in such circumstances financial advice and support; also offers support to neighbours in dispute.

Plymouth Women's Refuge: PO Box 53, Plymouth, PL3 4XQ. Tel: (01752) 558048 or (01752) 562286 Offer advice, information and support to people suffering domestic violence and abuse. Available 24 hours with limited use of an answerphone.

Women's Aid: 12 Oxford Avenue, Hyde Park, Plymouth, PL3 4SQ. Tel: (01752) 252033. Provide support, services and counselling for women and children who have suffered domestic abuse. This is a women only service.

ONE PARENT FAMILIES
Children and Lone Parents Ltd: 19 North Street, Plymouth, PL4 9AH. Tel: (01752) 201245. A self-help association for all parents bringing up children on their own, whether divorced, separated, widowed, unmarried or because one partner is seriously disabled or away from home for a long period due to hospitalisation, imprisonment, work or any other reason. Provides advice on legal and matrimonial problems, information and support at the North Street Centre. The Centre is open 9 am - 5 pm Monday to Friday. Anyone is welcome to drop in.

Cruse Bereavement Care: Tel: (01752) 408134 National helpline 0870 167 1677 A national charitable organisation set up to help all bereaved people, wherever they live, whatever their age, nationality and belief. Help of many kinds may be needed and Cruse gives this help through counselling, advice, support, information and opportunities for contact with others. Professional advice and assistance can be arranged on an individual basis at home. There is a weekly coffee morning and social evening; the group also arranges outings to shows, places of interest, etc

(See also Plymouth Local Information System for Parenting on page 86)

HEALTH SERVICES

GENERAL

Lists of local **National Health Service Family Doctors, Dentists, Pharmaceutical Chemists, Opticians**, giving addresses, surgery hours, etc are available from:

Plymouth Primary Care Trust, Building One, Derriford Business Park, Brest Road, Plymouth, PL6 5QZ   Tel : 01752 315315. The lists are also available through the Internet via www.parents-guide-to-plymouth.co.uk/advice.htm

You should contact your local Primary Care Trust for:
- Advice on local NHS services
- To make suggestions, comments or complaints about services
- Patient's charter standards
- Local support groups
- Hospital waiting times...
- Or any other issues relating to the health service.

If you need any of the following:
- A new medical card
- A prescription charge exemption certificate
- A prescription pre-payment certificate

you should contact the Patient and Practitioner Services Agency: PPSA, Cecil Boyall House, Southernhay East, Exeter, EX1 1RB.

Dentists

To find a dentist consult the Plymouth Primary Care Trust (address above) or follow the links at www.parents-guide-to-plymouth.co.uk/advice.htm. Free dental care is available to children and young people under l8 (under 19 if in full time education), to expectant mothers and to women who have had a baby in the past year (even if the baby was still-born or died during the year); to people who are entitled to, or are named on, a valid NHS tax credit exemption certificate, and to people who are getting (or their partner gets) income support or income-based jobseeker's allowance or MIG or have a valid HC2 certificate

Always check that your dentist is offering treatment under the National Health Service. Children should receive regular dental examinations from the ages of 2 - 3 years. Please note that if a dental appointment is made and not kept nor cancelled in advance, a charge will be made, even if the patient is exempt from treatment charges. Your own dentist is required to provide emergency treatment for patients registered with him/her. If you do not have a dentist and need emergency treatment, call the Dental Access Centre on (01752) 314151.

Family Doctors
Everyone is entitled to the services of a family doctor (also called general practitioner). Most doctors run their own ante-natal and child health clinics. To obtain the names of local doctors who provide such services consult the N.H.S. Medical List mentioned on page 101. Doctors also produce their own practice leaflet detailing all their services. It is worth bearing in mind that when a child has a simple illness, it may be much quicker for a parent to ask their local pharmacist for advice. They are usually able to offer appropriate medication and/or advice. If not they will obviously advise a visit to the doctor if necessary.

Prescriptions
Free prescriptions are available to children under 16 years (under 19 if still in full-time education); to pregnant women and mothers with babies under 12 months old, who have a valid exemption certificate; to pensioners; to people suffering from a listed medical condition or a continuing physical disability which means they cannot go out without help from another person and who have a valid exemption certificate; to people who are entitled to, or are named on, a valid NHS tax credit exemption certificate, and to people who are getting (or their partner gets) income support or income-based jobseeker's allowance or MIG or have a valid HC2 certificate

To apply for a maternity exemption certificate obtain Form FW8 from your doctor, midwife or health visitor. If you do not qualify for free prescriptions and need them often you may be able to save money with a prescription prepayment certificate (PPC). You can obtain an application form (Form FP95) from most pharmacies or telephone 0845 850 0030 to pay by credit/debit card. Chemists operate a rota of late-night, Sunday and Bank Holiday openings for the sale of medical goods and dispensing of prescriptions. Details are published in the local press and are available from NHS Direct on 0845 46 47, or go to www.parents-guide-to-plymouth.co.uk/advice.htm.

NHS Glasses
To find an optician consult the NHS list mentioned above. Free NHS eye examinations are available to the following groups of people:

- Children under 16 years or under 19 years if in full time training or education;
- People suffering from diabetes and glaucoma
- Close relatives of glaucoma sufferers (if aged 40 years or over)
- People requiring complex lenses.
- People holding a valid HC2 certificate

- People who are registered blind or partially sighted
- People who are entitled to, or are named on, a valid NHS tax credit exemption certificate
- People who are getting (or their partner gets) income support or income-based jobseeker's allowance or MIG

A free voucher for NHS glasses is available for children under 16 years or under 19 years if in full time training or education; also for those who are entitled to, or are named on, a valid NHS tax credit exemption certificate, and to people who are getting (or their partner gets) income support or income-based jobseeker's allowance or MIG or have a valid HC2 certificate
For further information see Leaflet HC11, available from hospitals, opticians, family doctors, dentists and Jobcentre Plus offices.

OTHER HEALTH SERVICES IN THE COMMUNITY
Health Visitors
Each family has a health visitor/public health nurse who can offer help and advice on a wide range of health promotion activities such as smoking cessation, healthy eating, promotion of exercise etc. The health visitor/public health nurse is able to offer home visits. One such visit would be to new mothers and babies between the 10th –14th day after delivery, the start of a relationship where together the health and development of your baby is monitored until school entry at 4 years old.

The health visitor/public health nurse can be contacted (for advice and information) at the doctor's surgery or child health clinic. Advice can be offered on baby's progress, breastfeeding, feeding and weaning, behaviour and sleep management, minor illnesses and family difficulties, which may be physical, social or emotional, including postnatal depression.

Child Health Clinics
The following clinics are held in various parts of Plymouth and are usually open one or two mornings/afternoons a week. Parents are welcome to pop into their local clinic without an appointment, to weigh their babies, to see their health visitor or to buy welfare babymilk. Check the opening times with your local clinic. The clinics are not intended for ill babies, who should be taken to the family doctor in the usual way. Appointments are made for parents to bring their babies to the surgery/clinic for vision and developmental checks and for vaccination, protecting against infectious diseases.

The **Plymouth Health Authority clinics** are located as follows and are available to sell baby milks at the times stated.

Brandreth Road Health Clinic, Plymouth Tel: (01752) 257256   9.30 am - 11.30 am Friday

Royal Naval Community Centre, Crownhill Road. Tel: (01752) 779765 10.00 am -12 noon Tuesday

Cumberland Centre, off Madden Road, Devonport. Tel: (01752) 566600 9.00 am-4.30 pm Monday, Tuesday, Wednesday, Thursday; 9.00 am – 4.00 pm Friday

Efford Community Centre, Blandford Road, Efford. Tel: (01752) 776853 9.30 am - 11.30 am Wednesday

Ernesettle Family Centre, Infants School, Biggin Hill, Ernesettle. 2.00 pm - 4.00 pm Tuesday

Estover Health Centre Leypark Walk, Estover. Tel: (01752) 788411 11.00 am -12.30 pm and 2.00 pm - 4.00 pm Tuesday and Thursday

Jan Cutting Healthy Living Centre, Scott Hospital, Beacon Park Road. Tel: (01752) 362256 2.00 pm - 4.00 pm Monday

Honicknowle Clinic, Honicknowle Green. Tel: (01752) 788407 2.00 pm - 4.00 pm Monday

Laira Clinic, Pike Road Surgery, Laira. Tel: (01752) 663473 2.30 pm - 4.30 pm Thursday

Plympton Clinic, Station Road, Plympton. Tel: (01752) 336527 (Not Health Centre) 2.00 pm - 4.00 pm and l0.00 am - 12 noon Monday and Wednesday

Plymstock Clinic, Horn Cross Road, Plymstock. Tel: (01752) 402677 2.00 pm - 4.00 pm Wednesday and Thursday
Roborough Recreation Hall, Roborough. 9.30 am - 11.30 am Thursday

St Budeaux Health Centre, Stirling Road, St Budeaux. Tel: (01752) 314838 10.00 am - 12 noon and 2.00 pm - 4.00 pm Monday and Friday

Seventrees Clinic, Baring Street, Greenbank. Tel: (01752) 260071 2.00 pm - 4.00 pm Monday, Tuesday, Thursday

Southway Clinic, Inchkeith Drive, Southway. Tel: (01752) 768696 2.00 pm - 4.00 pm and 9.30 am - 11.30 am Monday and Wednesday

Tamerton Foliot Clinic, Hill Top Community Centre, Cunningham Road, Tamerton. 1.30 pm - 3.30 pm Monday

Bethany Church Hall, Budshead Road, Whitleigh. 2.00 pm - 4.00 pm Wednesday

Baby milk is also available from clinics in the surrounding area at:

Ivybridge Health Centre, Station Road, Ivybridge. Tel: (01752) 690777 2.00 pm - 4.00 pm Tuesday and Thursday

Kingsbridge Health Centre, The Quay, Kingsbridge Tel: (01548) 853551 2.00 pm - 4.00 pm Wednesday

South Brent Health Centre, Plymouth Road, South Brent. Tel: (01364) 72394 2.00 pm - 4.00 pm Wednesday

Tavistock Clinic, 70 Plymouth Road, Tavistock. Tel: (01822) 615935. Available in clinic open hours

Yealmpton Health Centre (01752) 880650 2.00 pm - 4.00 pm Wednesday

Yelverton Health Centre, Available during clinic open hours (01822) 852202

Immunisation: The following immunisations are offered to young children: whooping cough, diphtheria, tetanus, poliomyelitis, hib and meningitis C, measles, mumps and rubella. These can be obtained through your general practitioner. If you are worried about your child being immunised do talk to your family doctor, health visitor/public health nurse about your fears.

Genetic Counselling: Genetic counselling is available to parents who have a child with a congenital disability and are considering having more children. They will receive advice and counselling regarding the chances of the next child being born with a similar disability. This service is available through a General Practitioner or Paediatrician.

Paediatric Podiatry Service: School children may be seen about any foot problems, e.g. ingrowing toenails, etc. Parents can contact the central Podiatry office at Seventrees Clinic. Tel: (01752) 255528

Plymouth Natural Health and Healing Centre: Unity House, 175 Outland Road, Plymouth PL2 3PY. Tel: (01752) 770048. Aims to encourage an interest in "holistic" living and provide free information on diet and nutrition, also taking into account mental and emotional states. They have lists of practitioners of alternative medicine such as homeopaths, chiropractors, reflexologists, etc. If your child requires a special diet the Natural Health Centre may be able to help, although they cannot promise to do so in every case. They will at least try to put you in touch with some one who can provide the necessary information. There is no charge for consultation, although donations are always welcome. Open 10.00 am to 4.00 pm Monday to Friday.

Speech and Language Therapy Service: Seventrees Clinic, Baring Street, Plymouth, PL4 8NF. Tel: (01752) 662221. Parents who are worried about their child's speech and language development can be referred to this service by their health visitor, clinic doctor or general practitioner, or they can contact the speech therapists at Seventrees Clinic directly. Speech therapists assess, diagnose and treat all types of speech and language defects and disorders in people of all ages. For children with problems the service offers advice to parents and treatment where necessary either individually or in a group. Clinics are held in a number of health centres and health clinics in West Devon.

Family Planning and Sexual Health Advisory Service
A service operating 14 family planning clinics in the Plymouth area. Confidential advice and guidance for all ages. Routine cervical smears; breast awareness – advice and teaching on self-examination. Telephone to book a pregnancy test. Time to talk about all sexual health matters to specialist staff. Cumberland Centre, Damerel Close, off Madden Road, Devonport, Plymouth, PL1 4JZ. Tel: (01752) 314661. See also Youth Enquiry Service page 87.

Patient Advice and Liaison Services (PALS): PALS aim to:
- advise and support patients, their families and carers;
- provide information on NHS services;
- listen to your concerns, suggestions or queries;
- help sort problems quickly on your behalf.

PALS act independently when handling patient and family concerns, liaising with staff, managers and, where appropriate, relevant organisations, to negotiate immediate solutions and to bring about changes to the way that services are delivered. If necessary, they can also refer patients and families to specific local or national-based support agencies. Tel: (01752) 211818. The PALS Co-ordinator is based at Plymouth Guild of Voluntary Service, Ernest English House, Buckwell Street, Plymouth, PL1 2DA.

Smoking Advice Service: There is a lot of support and advice available to help you, your partner and your family to give up smoking. The specialist service offers individual and group support sessions at Mount Gould or Derriford Hospitals or at your own home. Call the specialist service helpline on (01752) 314040.

HOSPITAL AND HEALTH FACILITIES FOR CHILDREN

Facilities are available for a parent to stay overnight with their child in the Plymouth Hospitals. Visiting hours are very flexible and where possible parents are encouraged to help care for their children. If a child is booked in advance for treatment, telephone before admission to check what facilities are available. Information leaflets are available for patients and families explaining the needs and requirements of a patient on admission. In some circumstances children may be able to visit the hospital before admission, please ring the ward to enquire.

Saturday Theatre Club – held on a Saturday morning and is open to children and their families to visit before coming in for a planned operation. Tel: (01752) 792928 for details of dates and times.

Currently, children are admitted to the following hospitals:

Derriford Hospital: level 12, Derriford Road– Tel: (01752) 777111 which offers good facilities for parents:

Woodcock Ward: babies and children up to 10 years: medical and surgical admissions. Tel: (01752) 792681

Whitehorse Assessment Unit: children's assessment unit: all emergency admissions. Tel: (01752) 792980

Wildgoose Ward: children and adolescents over 10 years old. Children of all ages for orthopaedic, diabetic and oncological care. Tel: (01752) 792048

Children's Day Beds: day cases, outpatient visits and tests. Tel: (01752) 763460

Playroom: situated on Woodcock Ward, staffed by play leaders, provides play, occupation, preparation and support for all children and their parents on level 12. Tel: (01752) 763476

Plym Day Case Unit: day case surgery ward. Tel: (01752) 792502

Transitional Care Ward: small or ill newborn babies not requiring intensive care. Tel: (01752) 763620

Neonatal Intensive Care Unit: for premature and sick babies needing special care. There are facilities if both parents wish to stay with their baby. Tel: (01752) 763600

Royal Eye Infirmary: Dale Road Mutley – Tel (01752) 315123. Casualty, outpatient and inpatient care for children with eye problems.

Child Development Centre: based at Scott Business Park (Beacon Park). This centre provides multi-professional outpatient care (e.g. medical, physiotherapy, speech and language, occupational therapy) and nursery provision for babies and children with developmental and special needs. Tel: (01752) 314352

Child and Adolescent Mental Health Service: based at Mount Gould Hospital. This service provides outpatient and day patient support for children and inpatient / day patient care for adolescents with emotional and behaviour difficulties. Tel: (01752) 272329

Children's Community Team: based on level 12 at Derriford Hospital. A team of children's nurses who support children who have ongoing health care needs, at home and in community settings. Tel: (01752) 763459

Paediatric Liaison: based on level 12 at Derriford Hospital. Provides a link between hospital, home and community staff. Tel: (01752) 763478

School Nursing: based at Mount Gould. School nurses help to meet the health needs of school age children, including immunisations, help with emotional or behaviour problems, health promotion, general problems e.g. hearing, continence etc. Tel: (01752) 272414

Plymouth Hospitals School: based on level 12 at Derriford Hospital. This is funded by the Local Education Authority and is responsible for providing education to those children unable to attend their own school because of health problems. Liaison is maintained with the child's own school and teacher. Teachers provide education in various locations within Plymouth, Mount Gould Hospital and occasionally in a child's home, according to individual need. Tel: (01752) 792476

Little Bridge House: Childrens Hospice South West: based in Barnstaple. Provides hospice care for children with life threatening / life limiting conditions. Tel: (01752) 321999.

Mustard Tree Macmillan Centre: based on level 3, Derriford Hospital. Support for relatives, and those dying from cancer. There is an associated support group for bereaved children, called Jeremiah's Journey. Tel: (01752) 763672/763671

MATERNITY SUPPORT
When you are first pregnant

Free pregnancy tests used to be available but most women are now expected to purchase a pregnancy testing kit from a pharmacy to do their own home test, although there are centres in Devonport that will carry out pregnancy tests (see page 113). It is very important for the health of the expectant mother and of her developing baby that she should visit her doctor as soon as she thinks she is pregnant. Community Midwives are attached to each family doctor's surgery/health centre. A mother-to-be will usually meet her Community Midwife at the surgery or by prior arrangement at home in early pregnancy.

The Plymouth Hospitals NHS Trust has produced the following information about Choices in Care:

When your Midwife comes to see you to talk to you about your pregnancy, medical and family history etc. she will also talk to you about the plans for your care. This will include who cares for you in your pregnancy and labour.

During your pregnancy you have these options:

Midwife Led Care: Care is provided by your Community Midwife together with your family doctor in your local surgery. The Community Midwife co-ordinates your care throughout pregnancy and labour (usually a hospital based midwife will provide care for you during labour).

Consultant Led Care: Care is provided by your Consultant Obstetrician at Derriford Hospital, together with your GP and Community Midwife in your local surgery. The Consultant Obstetrician co-ordinates your care throughout pregnancy and delivery working closely with your Community Midwife and Family Doctor.

For advice and support to quit smoking if you are pregnant, a partner or family or if you have recently had a baby and would like your home to be smoke-free call the

Smoking Advice Service

now on **01752 314040**

Free, confidential advice and support available from specialist advisers

Plymouth Teaching Primary Care Trust
South Hams & West Devon Primary Care Trust

NHS

The **Specialist Service** offers individual & group support sessions at **Mount Gould Hospital** or **Derriford Hospital** or at your own home.

You can also be supported by telephone. You are welcome to bring a friend or relative to the sessions.

Nicola says "I never believed I would be able to give up smoking as I'd tried everything, however I visited The Smoking Cessation Service, talked it through, set a date and quit. My husband was also able to access the service and we are now able to be non-smokers.

"The minute I stopped smoking I started to enjoy my pregnancy, without the guilt attached to smoking whilst pregnant, so thanks to smoking cessation."

The first option is available to women who have no medical problems or part obstetric difficulties and an uncomplicated pregnancy ie the majority! You may choose to have your baby at home or in hospital. You may choose to be cared for or have an appointment with a Consultant Obstetrician during your pregnancy even if you have no health problems or problems with your pregnancy. Some women prefer to do this before making their final choice on which type of care to have, or where to have their baby. If you have had any health problems or problems with previous pregnancies, your Midwife or GP will help you to decide which is the best option for you. You may also change your choice of care at any time during your pregnancy if another option becomes more suitable for you.

Parent Education Classes
The health centres and health clinics run regular classes to help mothers in the latter part of pregnancy prepare for childbirth. Limited Classes are also held at Derriford Hospital. There is an opportunity for all couples to attend a tour of the maternity wards. Mothers-to-be should ask their Community Midwife for details. (See also National Childbirth Trust below)

Sure Start Plus offers support, advice and information for all issues around pregnancy and parenting for young people under 18. Run a Young Parents' group, "before and after" the birth sessions for young parents; also offer help on a one to one basis. Sure Start Plus, Plymouth Foyer, 12-14 Octagon Street, Plymouth, PL1 1TU. Tel: (01752) 254597

National Childbirth Trust (NCT) The broad aim of the NCT is education for parenthood, which includes increasing awareness of the natural processes of pregnancy and childbirth and understanding of the medical assistance which is available for those who need it. It also realises the need for parents to explore and come to terms with their new role of parenting and caring for children. The National Childbirth Trust website can be accessed at www.parents-guide-to-plymouth.co.uk/matsup.htm and has advice and information on Pregnancy, Birth, After the Birth, Becoming a Dad, Child Development and much more. The Plymouth and West Devon Branch welcomes new members. Contact Sarah Jones on (01752) 661233 or email NCTplymouthandwestdevon@yahoo.co.uk

Where to Have Your Baby:
Maternity Unit, Derriford Hospital, Derriford Road, Plymouth, PL6 8DH. On the fifth floor of the hospital. Car park E is the closest to the entrance.

Facilities are available at Derriford for a waterbirth. Mothers wanting to use this method should discuss it with their Community Midwife, who will arrange a meeting with one of the Labour Ward Midwives.

Breastfeeding
The midwives in Plymouth give every encouragement and support to

breast-feeding mothers, as do the community health visitors. There are breastfeeding support groups in parts of the city, run by Sure Start, involving trained local parents, Sure Start midwives, local health visitors and community midwives:

Sure Start Plus at Plymouth Foyer Tel: (01752) 254597 (see page 111)
Sure Start Four Woods Tel: (01752) 366795 (see page 92)
Sure Start Keystone Tel: (01752) 312211 (see page 93)

For details of other groups that may be running in your area, contact your community midwife or health visitor.

The National Childbirth Trust website at www.nctpregnancyandbabycare.com has more information about breastfeeding and the Plymouth and West Devon NCT offers breastfeeding support (see page 111). For a list of places in Plymouth with facilities for breast-feeding mothers see page 18.

Advice on Reducing the Risk of Cot Death

Research continues into the causes and possible means of preventing cot death (otherwise known as sudden infant death syndrome). The Plymouth Hospitals NHS Trust Maternity Services Information booklet 2000 contains the following advice, which has resulted from considerable research into the possible causes of cot death.

- Lie your baby on his back to sleep.
- Avoid smoking during and after pregnancy and smoky rooms.
- Do not let your baby get too hot (or too cold). To check how warm your baby is, feel the tummy not hands and feet which often feel cold.
- Use thin layers of clothing and bedding that can be easily removed. When indoors babies over 4 weeks old do not need more clothes than their parents. The amount of bedding needed depends on the room temperature.
- Do not overheat your home - 65 °F (18 °C) is ideal for a baby.
- Remember to remove warm outdoor clothes when you take your baby indoors.
- Do not use duvets, cot bumpers or pillows for babies under 1 year old.

The midwife and health visitor will help parents who need further advice and it is worth remembering that cot death is rare.

The Stillbirth and Neonatal Death Society is a support group for parents who have suffered bereavement and they have compiled an advice section on their Website at www.sids.org.uk

Maternity Services Liaison Committee

A committee of maternity service users, health professionals and lay members responsible for advising on the commissioning of maternity services and the provision of maternity care. The aim of South & West Devon Maternity Services Liaison Committee (MSLC) is to ensure that the local users voice is heard and reflected in the planning and provision of maternity services whilst taking account of national policy and research. The MSLC is made up of health professionals (both from the hospital and community), voluntary groups such as the National Childbirth Trust, and parents with young children. It welcomes comments on the service, both directly and via panels of parents from different areas and backgrounds.

Westcountry Housing Association (Mother and Baby Project) 9 Lockyer Street, Plymouth, PL1 2QQ. Tel: (01752) 261602. A voluntary service providing supportive accommodation for young mothers. Women are able to be accommodated from six months pregnant onwards until the baby is one year old, provided they are between 16 and 30 years old.

Pregnancy Testing

The following centres will carry out pregnancy testing - you need to take a first morning urine sample in a clean bottle.

Twelves Company, 12 Cumberland Street, Devonport. Tel: (01752) 509605
Welcome Hall, 4 Fore Street, Devonport. Tel: (01752) 606317
Leander House, Fore Street, Devonport. Tel: (01752) 605174
Mount Wise Youth Project, 37d St Aubyn Street, Devonport. Tel: (01752) 606595
Plymouth Children's Information Service, 30 Marlborough Street, Devonport. Tel: (01752) 517480 or Freephone 0800 783 4259.

You can also book a pregnancy test with the Family Planning Service on (01752) 314661, although you will normally have to wait for an appointment (see page 107)

RELATIONSHIP GUIDANCE

Marriage Care South West: Plymouth & Cornwall Tel: 0771 323 4825. Provides free relationship counselling, particularly in times of crisis, pre-marriage training and schools visits, for anyone who would like to strengthen, mend or improve their relationship.

Relate, 3 Blenheim Road, North Hill, Plymouth, PL4 8LJ. Tel: (01752) 213131 Counselling for couples and individuals who are having relationship difficulties.

Appendix I Parents Guide to Plymouth on the Internet

The website www.parents-guide-to-plymouth.co.uk was launched in 2001 and provides a portal to many other websites of interest to parents, some local, some national and some international.

The website also offers up to date information on what's happening in the area, particularly those events aimed at children and/or families. Details of holiday and half term activities are also included, where supplied. To have your events included (free of charge), please send to Parent Friendly by post or email (contact details below).

The website message board enables you to add information of interest to parents, make and help with enquiries, or offer feedback about the site.

Important updates to the Parents Guide to Plymouth book are available at www.parents-guide-to-plymouth.co.uk/update.htm

If you don't have Internet access:

- Plymouth City Libraries offer free Internet access in all their Plymouth branches.
- UK online centres are for people who have limited or no access to new technologies. The centres will help people to develop the skills to use the Internet to access information and to send email. UK online centres are based in communities and will enable anyone in England who wants it, to have access to the Internet and e-mail. To find out where your nearest centre is telephone Learn Direct on (FREEPHONE) 0800 77 1234.
- Internet cafes in your local area offer access to the Internet for an hourly charge.

Parent Friendly always welcomes further information and ideas for inclusion on the website or in the book.

Contact Information:
By post: Parent Friendly, 21 Ernesettle Crescent, Plymouth, PL5 2ET
By e-mail: parentsguide@btinternet.com.

You've seen the book, now visit the website at:

www.parents-guide-to-plymouth.co.uk

and check out the comprehensive
What's on listings and Holiday activities

also check out and contribute to the
Message Board

Don't forget to watch out for
Updates to the book

 Do you have a business that is family-friendly? Notify Parent Friendly to be included on the website.

 Do you have a local family friendly business with a website? Contact Parent Friendly to arrange a weblink.

 Do you organise events for families in the Plymouth area? Send information for the What's On section.

e-mail: parentsguide@btinternet.com

UPDATE

Please amend the following entry on page .... of the 2004/2005 edition of A Parents Guide to Plymouth:

....

....

....

....

....

....

....

You may also use this page to notify Parent Friendly of information that you would like to see included in the next edition.

Name: ....

Address: ....

....

....

Photocopy this page if you do not want to cut your copy of the book.

Please notify me when the next edition is available: YES/NO

Post to: Parent Friendly, 21 Ernesettle Crescent, Plymouth, PL5 2ET